11th January 2005

Hamilton

Proceedings in the Court of Vice-Admiralty of Virginia

1698-1775

Edited by

George Reese

Virginia State Library
1983

Library of Congress Cataloging in Publication Data

Virginia. Court of Vice-Admiralty.
Proceeding in the Court of Vice-Admiralty of Virginia, 1698–1775.

Includes index.
1. Court records—Virginia. 2. Admiralty—Virginia. I. Reese, George Henkle. II. Virginia State Library. III. Title.
KF1111. V57 1983 347.755'04 83-1138
ISBN 0-88490-113-0 347.55074

Standard Book Number 0–88490–113–0.

Virginia State Library, Richmond, Virginia.
Printed in the United States of America.

FOREWORD

The publication of this slender volume of documents, edited by the experienced hand of George Reese, professor of humanistic sources at the University of Virginia, provides students of American history yet another bit of the time-, war-, and fire-ravaged archive of the colony of Virginia: the entire known extant corpus of the proceedings of the Virginia Court of Vice-Admiralty. The Virginia State Library is grateful to its sister institution, the Virginia Historical Society, for allowing the photographic reproduction on pages 59 through 115 of text published in the *Virginia Magazine of History and Biography*, LXXXVIII (1980), 301–337, LXXXIX (1981), 405–424. This made it economically feasible to publish these fragmentary historical records in one convenient volume with a single comprehensive index ably prepared by Susan Bracey Sheppard.

Jon Kukla

CONTENTS

PREFACE

THE three articles in this collection contain all known proceedings in cases tried by the Virginia Court of Vice-Admiralty, from its establishment until the collapse of the King's government put an end to the court. The articles also include references to other cases before the court, in 1698–1700, 1758, and 1770–1775, of which no records have come to light: it is probable that most of the court's papers were destroyed when the Capitol at Williamsburg burned in January 1747, or were scattered and lost about thirty years later during the American revolution.

I wrote these articles in the reverse of their order here, where they are so arranged that the proceedings are in chronological order. This accident of publication explains why a review of the colonial courts, with comment on the procedure and terminology of the courts, is found in the third article on pp. 80–82 below.

The articles presented here had no occasion to take into account whatever cases the Court of Vice-Admiralty had before it in 1701–1757 and 1759–1769; in consequence, they did not attempt to consider how many cases of those years may have left no official records. Although no proceedings in cases of 1701–1757 and 1759–1769 are known, the executive journals of the Council of colonial Virginia, in references to activities of the Court of Vice-Admiralty, suggest the nature of some of those cases; and the *Virginia Gazette* clearly points out the nature of some cases by advertisements for sales of ships and cargoes by decree of the court, or, rarely, in reports of a trial held or to be held in the court.

After the Court of Vice-Admiralty had been established for a few years, the Council's involvement in the affairs of the court evidently dwindled, for mentions in the Council journals of vice-admiralty business became infrequent. Still, the journals do allude to ten trials in the court, or to orders for the trials to be held, in the years 1706–1721. This figure excludes several trials for piracy by an admiralty court that the governor would have ordered, with the judge of vice-admiralty probably sitting as one of the members; in some of these trials and their aftermath other officers of the Court of Vice-Admiralty took part, the register on one occasion and the marshal several times. Three of those ten trials in the Court of Vice-Admiralty were for prosecution of French prize vessels, five were for illegal trading, one was for recovery of a debt owed for provisions and a supply of money, and one was evidently for trial of a vessel as a pirate, resulting in the condemnation of twenty–one Negro slaves as piratical effects. It is not certain that all the trials that were ordered were actually held, and usually the judgements of the court are unknown. Mentions of vice–admiralty business had become notably uncommon in the Council journals by 1721, and no mention is known of any date later than that year: it may be, then, that the missing journals, of May 7, 1754–June 10, 1756, September 15, 1763–September 5, 1767, and of any date after June 17, 1774, would have added little or nothing to what we know of the Court of Vice–Admiralty.[1]

The *Virginia Gazette* is in general a more fruitful source of information on the court than the Council journals are. The *Gazette,* founded in August 1736, began in 1745 to print notices or advertisements of the court's actions. From 1745 through 1769 the *Gazette* published one report of a court held to try a French prize vessel, and a dozen advertisements of sales by the court's decree of a variety of vessels, usually with their guns, rigging, tackle, apparel, and furniture, and often with their cargoes as well. The advertisements do not normally give the grounds for seizure and condemnation of the vessels; however, one advertisement does state that two vessels from Antigua were seized and condemned because they had not made entries of slaves they imported. Many similar advertisements are probably lost. The files of the *Gazette* are nearly complete for 1736–1739, but only seventeen issues of 1740–1765 are known, with none at all from 1741–1744, 1747–1750, 1758, 1760, and 1763.[2]

A few references to trials in vice–admiralty are supplied in correspondence, such as letters from Lieutenant Governor Francis Fauquier to his principal, Jeffery Amherst, with whom he shared the salary and miscellaneous income of the governorship. On March 5, 1760, Fauquier informed Amherst that they had profited by the confiscation of a flag of truce of Governor Denny's, presumably a cartel ship licensed by the governor of Pennsylvania, William Denny, seized and condemned in Virginia for illicit trading. Fauquier wrote again to Amherst on November 7, 1760, letting him know that he was remitting the value of £47, Virginia currency, as Amherst's share in the proceeds of a confiscated vessel. In 1761, Fauquier reported on July 8 that a vessel condemned in Virginia had produced £311.10.0, Vir-

[1] For the Council journals, see H. R. McIlwaine et al., editors, *Executive Journals of the Council of Colonial Virginia, 1680-1775* (Richmond, Va., 1925-1966).

[2] References in the *Virginia Gazette* will be found, under the entry "Admiralty court," in Lester J. Cappon and Stella F. Duff, *Virginia Gazette Index, 1736-1780* (Williamsburg, Va., 1950).

ginia currency, for their share. In 1763, Fauquier wrote on April 21 to Amherst that the Court of Vice–Admiralty had condemned two New England vessels engaged in contraband trade, and on May 9 he wrote again to tell Amherst that their share in the confiscation of those two vessels was £804.10.0, making Amherst's share £251.8.0 sterling at the current rate of exchange.[3]

Among the Admiralty Papers at the Public Record Office is a letter of March 17, 1771, from Benjamin Waller,[4] who had recently resigned his office as advocate of the Court of Vice–Admiralty, to an unidentified correspondent. In this letter Waller referred to three applications, all apparently of April–May 1769, for the holding of a Court of Vice–Admiralty. One application was by sailors hoping to recover their wages, one was by a customs collector for some purpose Waller did not mention, and one was by Captain Gell of the Royal Navy, who had seized a vessel. Gell's application at least was followed by a trial, for Waller remarked that he had had to carry on the prosecution alone because no lawyer would assist him, although several acted for the defense. The *Gazette* provides an unusual amount of information about this case. On April 13, 1769, the *Gazette* reported that Captain John Gell of H.M.S. *Launceston,* stationed in Virginia, had seized the snow *Nancy,* Richard Barron, master, from Lisbon; and on April 27 the newspaper published an advertisement that the snow *Nancy* was to be sold by decree of the Court of Vice–Admiralty.

The proceedings, or some part of the proceedings, in eighteen trials by the Virginia Court of Vice–Admiralty are known to exist. There are traces of fifty–three other cases, most and probably all of which were heard by the court, even if the proceedings in the trials have disappeared. One can only guess at how many cases, in addition to these seventy–one, came before the court. Possibly the missing Council journals, very probably the lacking issues of the *Virginia Gazette,* and perhaps the papers of colonial governors and other Virginia officials, still largely unexplored, would give evidence of cases in vice–admiralty of which we know nothing. And there were probably cases which would not as a rule have been noticed anywhere except in the records of the Court of Vice–Admiralty, such as those in which the vessels or cargoes on trial were acquitted and discharged, so that no sale was to be advertised, or maritime cases of interest only to the parties concerned, like a sailor's suit to recover his wages. What we know of this

---

[3] Fauquier's letters are in W.O. 34/37 ff. 34-35; Kent Archives Office, Maidstone, England, U 1350 052/1; and W.O. 34/37 ff. 79-80, 173, 174.

[4] The letter from Waller is in Adm. 1/3884 unnumbered pages.

Virginia court, then, relates in all likelihood to a small remnant of the cases heard in the court. We have the proceedings or parts of the proceedings for about a quarter of this remnant.

I am grateful to Her Majesty's Stationery Office for permission to publish documents from the Public Record Office in the first of the following articles. I thank the Virginia Historical Society for permitting me to reprint the other articles.

George Reese

University of Virginia

ABBREVIATIONS AND SHORT TITLES

AN	*The American Neptune*
CSPC	*Calendar of State Papers, Colonial Series. . . .* London, 1860–19—.
CSPD	*Calendar of State Papers, Domestic Series, of the Reign of William III. . . .* London, 1895–1937.
EJC	H. R. McIlwaine et al., editors, *Executive Journals of the Council of Colonial Virginia, 1680–1775.* Richmond, 1925–1966.
Hening	William Waller Hening, editor, *The Statutes at Large: Being a Collection of All the Laws of Virginia, from the First Session of the Legislature, in the Year 1619.* Richmond, Philadelphia, and New York, 1819–1823.
Md. Arch.	*Archives of Maryland.* Baltimore, 1883–19—.
P.R.O.	Public Record Office, London, repository of: Adm. Admiralty Papers C.O. Colonial Office Papers H.C.A. High Court of Admiralty Papers W.O. War Office Papers
Statutes	Owen Ruffhead, editor, *The Statutes at Large, from Magna Carta, to the End of the Last Parliament, 1761.* London, 1763–1800.
VMHB	*The Virginia Magazine of History and Biography.*

Proceedings in the Court of Vice-Admiralty of Virginia

1698-1775

THE COURT OF VICE-ADMIRALTY IN VIRGINIA 1696–1700

AMONG students of vice-admiralty courts in the North American colonies, common opinion was, and may still be, that all records of the Virginia Court of Vice-Admiralty have vanished.[1] Nevertheless, it is now evident that some of that court's records have survived.

The copies of proceedings in eight trials that follow are the earliest proceedings of the Virginia court, established in 1697/8, which are known to exist. They make up about one half of the court's records so far brought to light. The other records are the copy of proceedings in a single case of 1758, the trial and condemnation of a vessel seized for trading with the enemy; and a collection of forty-one original items from the period 1770–1775, the last six years of the court's existence. The records of 1770–1775, evidently a remnant of the court's archives, comprise the almost complete proceedings of the court in four cases; what appear to be the notes for the proceedings in a fifth case; thirty-three documents relating to proceedings in the group, but not incorporated in them; and three separate documents, each of which is all that remains of papers in the case to which it pertains.

No one in England appears to have called for reports of proceedings in the colonial courts of vice-admiralty, and nothing indicates that proceedings of those courts were often sent to England. It is true that Governor Nicholas Webb of the Bahamas sent to the Council of Trade and Plantations a copy of proceedings against a brigantine, the *Bahama Merchant,* in the court at New Providence on August 16, 1698; and Colonel Robert Quary, judge of the Court of Vice-Admiralty in Pennsylvania, sent to the Council copies of proceedings in his court on November 10–12, 1698 against the sloop *Jacob,* and on May 12–13, 1699 in the case of the *Providence.* These proceedings, however, were presumably submitted to the Council of Trade not simply for the Council's information: the Bahamas case, Webb thought, called for instructions from the Council; and the

---

[1] We are not concerned here with records of admiralty cases in Virginia courts before the Court of Vice-Admiralty was established in 1697/8. There is no way to determine how many such cases occurred, but there were at least two: one was the case of the *Fox,* in Lower Norfolk County court in 1647, the other was the case of the *Arms of Amsterdam,* in the General Court in 1664. See George Carrington Mason, "An Atlantic Crossing of the Seventeenth Century," *AN,* XI (1951) 35-41, and Kenneth Scott, editor, "The Arms of Amsterdam: An Extract from the Records of the General Court of Virginia, 1664," *VMHB,* LXXVII (1969), 407-440.

Pennsylvania cases exemplified some obstacles put in the way of the Court of Vice–Admiralty by provincial officials of Pennsylvania.[2]

Sir Edmund Andros, the governor of Virginia who appointed the first officers of Virginia's Court of Vice–Admiralty, sent no proceedings of trials in the new court, although there is evidence that two or perhaps three trials were held during the last months of his administration.[3]

Francis Nicholson, lately governor of Maryland, who succeeded Andros as governor of Virginia on December 9, 1698, wrote to the Council of Trade on February 4, 1698/9 from Jamestown, Virginia, reporting that on October 22, 1698 he had had the brigantine *Susannah* tried for illegal trading in the Court of Vice–Admiralty he had established in Maryland on January 11, 1697/8, and he enclosed the proceedings of the trial for no stated reason.[4]

At irregular intervals during the first three years of his administration, Nicholson transmitted to the Council of Trade and Plantations the records of proceedings in eight trials in the Virginia Court of Vice–Admiralty, printed below. It appears that these trials were all those (except one) that took place from the date of Nicholson's taking office as governor of Virginia, near the end of 1698, through 1700, the exception noted being the trial in about April or May 1699 of the *Integrity,* prosecuted and condemned for a breach of the acts of trade.[5] So far as one can tell, during the first years of the court its activities were regularly noted in the executive journal of the Council of Virginia, and that journal indicates that only these nine trials were held in 1699–1700. Why Nicholson did not send the proceedings against the *Integrity* has not been ascertained. Nicholson sent no proceedings of the court after he had sent those of 1699 and 1700 with his letters of June 10, and August 27, 1700 and of December 2, 1701.[6]

The proceedings Nicholson did send to the Council of Trade are copies prepared by or for the court and signed as a rule by the judge and the

---

[2] Abstracts of correspondence on these proceedings in the Bahamas and Pennsylvania are in *CSPC*, XVII, 52-55, 83-85, 235-237.

[3] See pages 7-8 below.

[4] Nicholson's letter and the proceedings are now in C.O.5/1309, ff. 206-213, 216-220. The letter is abstracted at length and the proceedings are briefly noted in *CSPC*, XVII, 47-51.

[5] The case of the *Integrity* is known only through brief mentions in *EJC*, I, 431, 464, II, 11.

[6] There is no evidence that the court sat during Nicholson's administration after October 19, 1700, when it heard the case of the *St. Peter & Anthony,* for which see pages 49-57 below. On August 14, 1702, the Council referred to the attorney general a petition of certain mariners, praying condemnation in a court of admiralty of rigging and stores from their vessel, in order to recover their wages. On August 17 the attorney general reported his opinion that the petitioners should take "the ordinary Process in the Court of Admiralty for their Relief," whereupon the governor and Council ordered the petitioners to apply to the judge of the admiralty court, who was to "give directions for issuing the usual Process" according to the attorney general's report; however, there is no further mention of the matter. See *EJC*, II, 267-268.

register. They are now among the Colonial Office Papers in the Public Record Office, London. Calendars of these papers published in the period 1905–1910 list the proceedings as enclosures with Nicholson's letters.[7] However, Charles M. Andrews did not mention them in his *Guide to the Materials for American History, to 1783, in the Public Record Office of Great Britain* (Washington, D.C., 1912–1914), and Andrews later wrote, in his essay "Vice–Admiralty Courts in the Colonies," that all records of the Virginia Court of Vice–Admiralty had vanished.[8] It does not appear that his statement was ever questioned.

The text of the manuscript copies of proceedings has been transcribed with a few changes. Superscript letters are brought down to the line. Long *s* is printed as short *s*, the letter *thorn* as *th*, and *m* or *n* under a horizontal dash as *mm* or *nn*. The noun–ending *–con* is rendered as *–tion*. A *p* with a crossed descender is printed as *pur–*, *pro–*, or *pre–*, as appropriate, and as *pas–* in the word *passenger,* where the scribe occasionally used the crossed *p*. Spelling, capitalization, and punctuation of the original are retained, although a full stop is supplied at the end of a paragraph if there was none. Abbreviations and contractions are retained, except that the various short forms of words designating the parties in a case, such as *complainant, defendant,* and *respondent,* are expanded without comment, and a few Latin words, names, and titles of office have been expanded with brackets. The erratic and wasteful spacing and margins of the originals have been altered for the sake of intelligibility and economy; most of the indentations have been supplied. When there is no doubt that a letter or word was left out simply by mistake, it is supplied in brackets. Doubtful readings and other textual problems are the subject of footnotes. All citations of the original texts refer to manuscripts in the Public Record Office. Transcriptions have been made from photographic copies of the original manuscripts.

On July 27, 1696, the Council of Trade and Plantations read a representation from the Commissioners of the Customs, recommending the establishment of a court of vice–admiralty in each colony as a means of enforcing the acts of trade and navigation and regulating the plantation trade. Four days later, the Council of Trade received a list of persons whom the Customs commissioners proposed as officers of the new colonial courts. Those named for Virginia were Edward Hill, judge, Miles Cary, register, Michael Sherman, marshal, and Edward Chilton, advocate. In fact, the

[7] *CSPC*, XVIII, 307-311, 313, 318-319, 496-499, XIX, 640-643, 655.

[8] The essay is the introduction to Dorothy S. Towle, editor, *Records of the Vice–Admiralty Court of Rhode Island, 1716–1752* (Washington, D.C., 1936).

list named Chilton as attorney general, for the Customs officials intended that in each colony one person should hold the offices of attorney general and of advocate of the Court of Vice–Admiralty.[9]

Nearly two years passed before the Admiralty sent out commissions and instructions for appointing officers in colonial courts of vice–admiralty. Sir Edmund Andros, governor of Virginia, received his commission, along with instructions as to whom he should appoint for the courts, on March 3, 1697/8. He wrote on March 14 to inform the Council of Trade and Plantations that, in obedience to the instructions, he had issued commissions to Edward Hill as judge and Miles Cary as register; he had sent for Michael Sherman, who was to be marshal; and he was awaiting the arrival of Edward Chilton, who was to be advocate.[10]

The commissions to Hill, Cary, and Sherman were dated March 8, 10, and 23 respectively. Andros issued a commission as advocate on March 23 to John Taylor, rather than to Chilton. It is not clear for what reason or by what authority Andros deviated from his instructions; he did not comment on the appointment, and the instructions have not been found.[11]

Little is known of the four officers beyond their various official appointments. Edward Hill is better defined than the others, because his vigorous support of the governor during Bacon's Rebellion provoked complaints of his behavior, earned him the disfavor of the commissioners sent to Virginia to investigate the uprising, and led him to write a defense of his conduct.[12] He was the most eminent of the four officers by virtue of being one of the twelve members of His Majesty's Council in Virginia, who were the governor's advisers, the upper house of the legislature, and the judges of the General Court, the colony's supreme court. He had been a justice of the peace, attorney general of Virginia, a member and speaker of the House of Burgesses, or lower house of the legislature, and treasurer of the colony. When he became judge of the Court of Vice–Admiralty he was collector and naval officer for the upper district of James River, and commander in chief of his county's militia. Miles Cary was commander in chief of militia in his county, and surveyor general of Virginia; he had been clerk of the

---

[9] In the 1690s, English officials referred to the courts simply as courts of admiralty, the term applied to them in Virginia also until some time in the eighteenth century. This study follows present usage in calling them courts of vice–admiralty. The representation and list from the Customs are in C.O.323/2 ff. 15-16, 22-23. Those and many other documents concerning the courts are abstracted in *CSPC;* for the courts through 1700 see volumes XV–XVIII.

[10] A copy of the commission to Andros, dated June 26, 1697, is in H.C.A.50/6 ff. 188-189. The letter from Andros to the Council of Trade is in C.O.5/1309 ff. 134-135.

[11] Copies of the four commissions are in C.O.5/1310 ff. 52-54.

[12] Hill's defense is printed in *VMHB,* III (1895), 239-252, IV (1896-1897), 1-15.

General Court and a member of the House of Burgesses. John Taylor had been both an officer of the militia and a member of the House of Burgesses, and was clerk of the court of Charles City County. Michael Sherman had been a justice of the peace, a militia officer, and a member of the House of Burgesses. All officers of the new court, then, were well established figures in the administration of Virginia, and all of them had practical experience of courts,[13] although nothing suggests that any of them had formal training in the law.

On March 10, 1697/8, Edward Hill took "the Oath of a Judge."[14] No record that the other officers took their oaths has been found, but it seems likely that they were sworn in as soon as possible after they received their commissions.

The first case before the new court was evidently that of the ship *Flying Hart,* a prize taken from the French in the West Indies and sold to Robert Beckford and Captain Willis Wilson (the former not identified, the latter probably a sea captain of King and Queen County in Virginia). On March 10, 1697/8 the Council, considering Beckford's request to have the ship admitted to trade after a Court of Vice–Admiralty had condemned her, decided the ship must be condemned before any other action could be taken. By April 13, 1698 the Court of Vice–Admiralty had condemned the ship, and upon a petition from Wilson the Council ordered that the ship and her furniture be delivered to him and the other owners, upon his giving security of £500 sterling to meet any claims against the ship as a capture and prize.[15]

A few days later, on April 21, 1698, in reply to a petition of James Perryman, master of the ship *Seventh Son,* the Council gave its opinion that Peter Heyman, collector for the lower district of James River, who had seized the ship, should immediately bring her to trial.[16] Neither the grounds for the seizure, nor any other mention of a trial, has come to light.

At the meeting of April 26, 1698, the Council dealt with another case of

---

[13] Hill had acted as judge of an admiralty court, having been commissioned on June 12, 1697 to try a prize ship. This information, like nearly all information on courts of admiralty and vice–admiralty in Virginia outside of the surviving court records, is found in *EJC*. For Hill's commission on this occasion see *EJC,* I, 366-368.

[14] *EJC,* I, 379.

[15] *EJC,* I, 380-381. A foreign–built ship, legally condemned as a prize in a court of admiralty in England, Ireland, or the plantations, could be made free or naturalized so as to enjoy the advantages of an English–built ship. The security was probably required to meet such claims as the King's share in a prize ship, and any shares allowed to the captor or captors or others, if not already paid. See Charles M. Andrews, *The Colonial Period of American History* (New Haven and London, 1938), IV, 78, 80, 160, 172, 237.

[16] *EJC,* I, 383.

a prize ship and its condemnation. Captain Henry Jenkins (who was probably a sea captain of Elizabeth City County and then of York County in Virginia) presented a petition concerning the ship *St. Louis* of Martinique, captured in the West Indies, brought to Virginia, sold to Jenkins, and condemned by a court of vice–admiralty in Virginia. In reply to his petition, the Council ordered the ship and her furniture to be delivered to Jenkins, he giving security of £100 sterling to meet any claims upon the ship as a capture and a prize.[17]

The earliest case before the Virginia Court of Vice–Admiralty for which the proceedings have been found is the suit of three mariners to recover their wages from John Neal, master of the ship *Mary Ann*. The case was perhaps the first heard by the court since Andros had been succeeded as governor of Virginia, on December 9, 1698, by Francis Nicholson, who sent a copy of the proceedings with his letter of June 10, 1700 to the Council of Trade and Plantations. This is the record of the proceedings:[18]

At the Court of Admiralty held at James City on Wednesday the 22d: day of Febry. in the Eleventh year of the Reign of our Sovereign Lord William the third by the Grace of God of England Scotland France & Ireland King Defender of the faith Annoq. Dom: 1698.[19]

Before the Honble: Edward Hill Esq. Judge of the Sd. Court.

Thomas Knuckle Thomas Hilsey and Thomas Paul Mariners of and belonging to the Ship Mary Ann of Plymouth Alledgeing & Complaining That upon the tenth day of Janry. in the year of our Lord 1697 at the Port of Bristoll in the Kingdom of England they were by John Neal Master of the Sd. Ship Mary Ann hyred and Imployed as Mariners to Saile and work on board the Sd. Ship in maner following that is to Say the Sd: Thomas Knuckle to be Mate of the Sd Ship and to receive Wages after the rate of three pounds ten Shill: Sterl: for every Kallender moneth he Should Continue in that Service the Sd. Thomas Hilsey to be Carpenter of the Sd Ship and to receive wages after the rate of three pounds ten Shill: Sterl: for every Kallender moneth he Should Continue in that Service and the Sd. Tho: Paul to be Boatswain of the Sd. Ship and to receive Wages after the rate of two pounds ten Shill: Sterl: for every Kallender moneth he Should Continue in that Service and That the Sd. Jno: Neal at the Expence of the Said Ship According to the Custome of the Sea in Such Cases Should provide them the Sd: Mariners wth: Necessary diet & other Conveniencies & that over & above the afore mentioned Wages the Sd. Jno: would allow the Sd. Tho: Knuckle the priviledge of haveing three Tuns of Salt for his own use without paying any freight the Said Ship being

[17] *EJC*, I, 383.

[18] The proceedings are in C.O.5/1311 ff. 122-124.

[19] James City was another name for Jamestown, then the capital of Virginia. Dates in these proceedings follow the old system, in which a new year began on March 25. The trial opened on February 22, 1699, by our present calendar.

then bound on a Voyage from the Port of Bristoll aforesd to the Isle of May & thence to this Colony of Virga:[20]

And that Pursueant to the Agreemt: So made with them by the Sd. John they did goe on board the Sd. Ship & According to their Several Stations did their duties there & So Continued ready at all times to do until the tenth day of Febry: in the year of our Lord 1698 in which Space are Contained thirteen Kallender moneths So that thereby becomes due to the Sd. Mariners for Wages the Sum of one hundred twenty three pounds ten Shill: Sterl: That is to Say forty five pounds ten Shill: Sterling to the Sd. Tho: Knuckle forty five pounds ten Shill: Sterl: to the Sd. Tho: Hilsey & thirty two pounds ten Shill: Sterl: to the Sd: Tho: Paul and to the Sd. Tho: Knuckle is due the further Sum of Seven pounds Sixteen Shill: Sterl: for the afore mentioned priviledge of Salt & that upon the 12th: day of Novemr. last past he the Sd: Jno: did refuse to Provide or give Necessary Diet as aforesd to the Sd. Mariners So that they have been Necessitated to be at great Expences to Provide Diet & other Conveniencies as aforesd for them Selves whereby they have Expended thirty Six pounds Sterl: of their own money That is to Say each of them hath Expended twelve pounds Sterl: and that he will not Imploy them on board the Sd. Ship that they may Perform their Voyage & Obtain their Wages in England neyther will he pay them their Wages which are already due to them that they may be at liberty to go about their Lawfull Occations but hath recd very Sufficient Effects by the Profits of the Voyage from the Port of Bristoll to the Isle of May and thence to this Countrey which Sd Effects he the Sd. John is Sending out of this Countrey and is about to haul his Sd. Ship on Shoar & So to leave the Sd. Mariners without remedy for their Wages and other their Demands aforesd: therefore they the Sd. Mariners Do humbly pray That he the Sd. Jno: Neal Master as aforesd. may be Compelled to pay them the Sum of one hundred Sixty Seven pounds Six Shill: Sterl: in maner as before Expressed for Wages priviledge of Salt & Expences for diet and other Conveniencies Since the 12th: day of Novemr: last with reasonable Costs and Charges for the delay and trouble of this prosecution.

To which the Defendant Jno: Neal Appeard and by his Council moveing that the Complainants might enter into Stipulation or bond wth: Sureties for the paymt: of Such damages Costs & Fees that might Accrue & Should be Decreed agt: them the Sd. Complainants And likewise the Sd. Complainants praying that the Said Defendant Should enter into like Stipulation or bond wth: Sureties for payment of Such part of their Wages Costs & Fees that might or Should be Decreed agt: him the Sd. Defendant which being reciprocally done Accordingly and the defendant praying time till to morrow morning to answer the Sd Lybel [of] Complaint the Same was granted and the Court adjourn'd til Thursday morning eight a Clock at which time being met the Defendant put in the following answer to the Sd. Libel of Complaint.

That is to say That the Sd. Tho: Knuckle Tho: Hilsey & Tho: Paul on the

---

[20] The Isle of May must have been the island of Maio, one of the Cape Verde Islands off the west coast of Africa. Salt is a principal export of the island, where the ship probably called to take on her cargo, identified as salt in the defendant's answer to the libel of complaint.

twentieth day of Augt: last past in Company with Severall other Mariners belonging to the Sd. Ship Mary Ann did unlawfully absent themselves from & desert the Service of the Sd. Ship wth:out the leave and against the Consent of the Said Respondant for the Space of many days whereby the Sd. Ship & her Ladeing Sustained great loss & Damage the Sd. Respondant not being Capeable of disposeing & Delivering the Lading of the Sd. Vessel (the Same being Salt) for want of the due & Necessary Assistance of the Sd. Complainants & the rest of the mariners they Seduced wth: them So that by the Law Marine no Wages ought to be paid to all or any of the Sd: Complainants after Such desertion & that the Sd Mary Ann was bound from Bristoll to the Isle of May & from thence hither & So to England again which Sd. Voyage they the Sd. Complainants did refuse to Serve out & Accomplish & did Spread abroad & report many false & feigned Reports & words of the Sd Ship as that She was rotten and unable to fulfill her Voiage and did refuse to do any thing to her thô thereunto required by the Sd Respondent by reason of which false Speeches & Suggestions all Persons have been affraid & have refused to Venture to freight any Tobacco or other Merchandizes on board the Said Ship whereby this respondent has utterly lost his Voyage home and is made incapeable of Complying with his owners Express Order of fiting his Sd Ship for that purpose which he did intend to do and that he did not refuse to allow and Provide the Sd. Complainants their Necessary Dyet before they deserted the Service of the Sd Ship & Saveing to himself all Exceptions to the many untruths & manifest falshoods Exhibited and Set forth by the Sd. Complainants in their Said Libel of Complaint prayeth that he may be dismissed from any further Prosses in this Honble: Court and that the Sd. Complainants by Decree of this Honble: Court may be Compel'd to pay the respondent his reasonable Costs & Damages besides all fees & Charges.

Which being Argued on both Sides & Severall Evidences Sworn & Examined the Court for the further Consideration thereof Adjourn'd to fryday eight a Clock at which time being met and haveing duely weighed & Considered the Premisses & it not Appearing that the Complainants deserted the Service of the Sd. Ship on or about the 20th: of August last past as by the Respondent is Set forth but that the Sd Complainants return'd on board the Sd. Ship in four or five dayes (after haveing made Complaint to a Magistrate) and there Continued & was recd in the Sd. Ship by the Sd Respondent and Performed their Duty on board till the xiith of Novemr: last past at wch: time the Sd Respondent denyed to Provide & give Necessary Dyet to the Sd. Complainants & the Sd Respondent Acknowledgeing That the Sd. Tho: Knuckle as Mate was to receive Wages after the rate of three pounds ten Shill: Sterl: for every Kallender Moneth he Should be in the said Service and the Sd. Tho: Hilsey as Carpenter to receive Wages after the Rate of three pounds ten Shill: Sterl: for every Kallender Moneth he Should be in the Said Service and the Sd. Tho: Paul as Boatswain to receive Wages after the rate of two pounds ten Shill: Sterl: for every Kallender moneth he Should be in the Sd Service and further that the Sd. Tho: Knuckle Should have the Priviledge of one Tun of Salt for his own Use without paying any freight and there being Contained ten Kallender moneths & two days from the Sd. tenth of Janry. 1697 to the Sd. twelfth of Novemr: 1698 So that thereby there becomes due to the Sd. Mariners for Wages as aforesd the Sum of Ninety five pounds twelve Shill: eight pence Sterl: that is to Say thirty five pounds four Shill: eight pence Sterl: to the Sd. Tho: Knuckle thirty five pounds four Shill: eight pence Sterl: to the Sd. Tho: Hilsey twenty five pounds three Shill: four pence Sterl: to the Sd. Tho: Paul & to the Sd Tho: Knuckle the further Sum of one pound Seventeen Shill: Six pence for his Priviledge of Salt as aforesd.

It is therefore Considered adjudged & Decreed and the Sentence of the Court is That the Sd. Respondent Jno: Neal Master of the Sd Ship Mary Ann pay unto the Sd. Mariners the Sum of Ninety Seven pounds ten Shill: two pence Sterl: that is to Say to the Sd Thomas Knuckle for his Wages & priviledge of Salt as aforesd thirty Seven pounds two Shill: two pence to the Sd. Tho: Hilsey for his Wages thirty five pounds four Shill: eight pence and to the Sd. Tho: Paul for his Wages twenty five pounds three Shill: four pence wth: Costs Fees & Charges which Sd. Costs Fees & Charges are as followeth that is to Say to the Judge four pounds Seventeen Shill: Six pence to the Register two pounds eight Shill: Nine pence and to the Marshal two pounds eight Shill: nine pence.[21]

Edw: Hill

On February 25, 1698/9, according to the journal of the Council, Hill, Cary, Taylor, and Sherman took their oaths as officers of the Court of Vice-Admiralty. It is not clear why Hill, and perhaps the other officers, had to be sworn in a second time. However, it is clear that the oaths were taken by Governor Nicholson's direction.[22]

And on February 25, 1698/9, the Council ordered Hill to take the tackle, apparel, and furniture belonging to H. M. advice boat *Swift* and ketch *Roe,* both wrecked, and have them sold at public sale.[23]

At an undetermined date, probably about April 1699, Peter Heyman seized the ship *Integrity* of Bideford, Aaron Whitson master; she was prosecuted in the Court of Vice-Admiralty by the attorney general (Bartholomew Fowler, appointed on October 29, 1698), and condemned for breach of the acts of trade. Whitson asked to be granted an appeal to the High Court of

21 These fees were percentages of the amount the respondent was ordered to pay: the judge took five percent, the register and marshal each took two and a half percent. The Council suggested the amount of the fees on February 24, 1698/9 (the day the sentence of the court was delivered), answering Edward Hill's representation that no fees had been settled for officers of his court in proceedings on private causes. *EJC,* I, 413.

22 The taking of the oaths, with their wording, is recorded in *EJC,* I, 413-414. On July 1, 1699 Nicholson wrote to the Council of Trade and Plantations, transmitting a copy of the commissions from Andros to Hill, Cary, Sherman, and Taylor, whom he supposed Andros had orders to appoint, although he had found no such orders. Nicholson added that the commissions were from Andros, but the oaths of office, of which he sent copies, were his own. For the letter and enclosures see C.O.5/1311 ff. 12-31, 53-55.

23 Hill was assisted by Cary and Sherman. On their requesting allowances for their trouble and expenses, the Council ordered that Hill should have £5 sterling for ten days of attendance, Cary £1.16.0 sterling for six days, and Sherman £2.8.0 sterling for eight days. *EJC,* I, 415, II, 6.

Admiralty, but after Edward Hill had the vessel appraised, Whitson offered to buy her at the appraised value and drop his appeal. Hill thereupon sought the advice of governor and Council who, on May 5, 1699, advised him that Whitson should be allowed to buy the vessel at the appraised value, provided Heyman raised no objection.[24]

No particulars of the sale are known. On June 22, the Council ordered payment to the attorney general of £5 sterling, from the proceeds of the sale of the *Integrity,* as his fee for prosecuting the ship. On October 18, the Council journal recorded that the ship had been appraised, that the owners were authorized to purchase her at the appraised value, and that Governor Nicholson had decided that of his share in the proceeds from the sale he would give one half to the College of William and Mary and remit the other half to the ship's owners.[25]

On June 7, 1699, while the disposal of the *Integrity* was evidently still being negotiated, Hill presented a petition from the four officers of the Court of Vice–Admiralty to the governor, stating that their outlay in attending the court was much greater than their fees and profits, on which account they asked the governor to recommend the establishing of salaries for the officers of the court.[26] Nicholson sent a copy of the petition with his letter of July 1, 1699 to the Council of Trade, and in the letter proposed annual salaries of £50 for the judge, £25 for the register and for the advocate, and £20 for the marshal, all to be paid from the tax of two shillings per hogshead on tobacco exports, or else from the quitrents. Neither the petition nor the governor's recommendation had any perceptible effect, and the officers of the court never enjoyed regular salaries.

Condemnation of the *Integrity* was followed by another prosecution for violation of the acts of trade. On June 22, 1699 the governor and Council considered a letter from Gawin Corbin, collector of the district of Rappahannock River, reporting his seizure on June 20 of the *Providence* of Dublin for illegal importation of goods from Ireland and asking for the governor's instructions respecting trial of the ship. The governor and Council thereupon ordered a trial in a Court of Vice–Admiralty at the court house of

---

[24] *EJC,* I, 431-432. The journal gives the place name as Biddeford, like that of the coastal town in Maine, but it is more likely the port was Bideford, in Devonshire.

[25] *EJC,* I, 464, II, 11. The journal does not suggest why the attorney general prosecuted, whether he acted with the advocate, or in his place. The act of 15 Charles II, c. 7, *An Act for the Encouragement of Trade,* provided that one third of the proceeds of a forfeited vessel, fittings, and cargo should go to the King, one third to the governor of the colony where the ship was tried, and one third to the informer. The act is printed in *Statutes,* III, 267-271.

[26] *EJC,* I, 449.

Middlesex County on July 12, with the officers of the court in attendance and the attorney general prosecuting on behalf of the King.[27]

The trial of the *Providence* began as ordered on July 12, except that, as the following proceedings suggest, the advocate appeared as prosecutor, with the attorney general presumably acting as additional counsel for the prosecution:[28]

Att the Court of Admiralty Held att the Court House for Middlesex–County on the 12th day of July in the Eleaventh year of the Reign of our Sovereign Lord William the third by the Grace of God of England Scotland France and Ireland King Defender of the Faith &c: Annoq Dom: one thousand Six hundred Ninety Nine.

Before the Honble: Edward Hill Esqr Judge of the sd Court.

Came John Taylor his Majtyes Advocate and Exhibited an Information against the Ship Providence of Dublyn John Hamelton Master at the Suit of Gowin Corbyn Esqr: Collector of his Majtyes Customs in the Port of Rappahannock.[29]

Which sd Information is as followeth Vizt

Virga: ss
Cur: Adm: July 11th. 1699 Ano: 11o: Gul. 3. &c

To the Honble: Court of Admiralty Gowin Corbyn Esqr as well for and in behalf of his Majty King William his Excy: Francis Nicholson Esqr: his Majtyes Lieut: and Govr: Genll: of Virga: as for and on behalf of himself gives this Court to Understand and be Informed

That by one Act of Parliament made the 15th year of King Charles the Second Entituled An Act for the Incouragement of Trade[30] It is by one Clause in the sd Act Enacted "That from and after the 25th day of March 1664 No Commodyty of the Growth Production or Manufacture of Europe Shall be Imported into any Land Island Plantation Colony Territory or Place to his Majty belonging or which Shall hereafter belong unto or be in the Possession of his Majty his heirs and Successrs in Asia Africa or America (Tangier only Excepted) But what Shall be Bona fide and without Fraud Laden and Shipped in England Wales or [the] Town of Berwick upon Tweed and in English Built Shiping or which were Bona fide Bought before the first day of October 1662 and had Such Certificate thereof as is directed in one Act passed the last Session[s] of this present Parliament Entituled An Act for preventing Frauds and Regulating Abuses in his Majtyes Customs and whereof the Master and three fourths of the Mariners at least are English

[27] *EJC,* I, 458. Middlesex County lies on the south side of the Rappahannock River, extending into Chesapeake Bay.

[28] The proceedings are in C.O.5/1311 ff. 129-135; Governor Nicholson transmitted them with his letter of June 10, 1700 to the Council of Trade and Plantations.

[29] The port of the district of Rappahannock River was at Urbanna, in Middlesex County; Corbin's residence was in the same county, a short distance up the river from Urbanna.

[30] The clauses quoted in this and the following paragraph are 6 and 8 of the act cited in note 25. The act mentioned in clause 6 is 13 & 14 Charles II, c. 11. *Statutes,* III, 236-243. Words and letters in brackets are in the printed act but not in this copy. Words in brackets, preceded by "*Act:*", give the text of the printed act if it differs from that of this copy.

and which Shall be Carryed directly thence to the sd Lands Islands Plantations Colonyes Territoryes or Place[s] and from no other Place or places whatsoever any Law Statute or Usuage to the contrary Notwithstanding Under the penalty of the Loss of [all] Such Commodytyes of the Growth Production or Manufacture of Europe as Shall be Imported into any of them from any other place whatsoever by Land or Water and if by Water of the Ship or Vessel Also in which they were Imported with all her Guns Tackle Furniture Amunition & Apparel one third part to his Majty his heirs & Successrs one third part to the Governr: of such Land Island Plantation Colony Territory or Place in which Such Goods were Imported If the sd Ship or Vessel [*Act*: Ship Vessel or Goods] be there Seized and Informed against or Sued for or otherwise that third part also to his Majty his heirs and Successors and the other third part to him or them who Shall Seize Inform or Sue for the Same In any of his Majtyes Courts in Such of the sd Lands Islands Plantations Colonyes [*Act*: Colonies, Plantations] Territoryes or Place[s] where the Offence was Committed or in any Court of Record in England by Bill Information Playnt or other Action wherein No Essoign Protection or Wager in [*Act*: of] Law shall be allowed."

And by one other Clause in the sd Act It is Enacted "That no Ship or Vessel Comeing to any Such Land Island Plantation Colony Territory or Place Shall Lade or Unlade any Goods or Commodytyes whatsoever untill the Master or Commander of Such Ship or Vessel Shall first have made known to the Govr: of Such Land Island Plantation Colony Territory or Place or Such other Person or Officer as Shall be by him thereunto Authorized and appoynted the Arrival of the sd Ship or Vessel with her Name and the Name & Sirname of the [*Act*: her] Master or Commander and have Shewn to him that She is an English Built Ship or made good by producing Such Certificate as abovesd That She is a Ship or Vessel Bona fide belonging to England Wales or the Town of Berwick and Navigated with an English Master and three fourth parts of the Mariners at least English Men and have delivered to Such Governr: or other Person or Officer a true and perfect Inventory or Invoyce of her Lading together with the Place or places in which the sd Goods were Laden or taken into the sd Ship or Vessel under the payn of the Loss of the Ship or Vessel with all her Guns Amunition Tackle Furniture and Apparel and of all Such Goods of the Growth Production or Manufacture of Europe as were not Bona fide Laden and taken in In England Wales or [the] Town of Berwick to be recovered and divided in manner aforesd.

Notwithstanding which one John Hamelton Master of the Ship Providence of Dublyn Burthen about one hundred and Sixty Tons now Riding at Anchor in Rappa: River did on or about the 30th of March last past Contrary to the before Recited Statute or Act Import in the sd Ship Providence into Middlesex–County in this his Majtyes Colony and Dominion of Virga divers Commodytyes of the Growth Production and Manufacture of Europe which were Laden & taken on Board the sd Ship in the Kingdom of Ireland and brought directly from thence hither without Cocquets (Vizt.) Seven Sets of Kedderminster Curtins and Vallians[31]

---

[31] These were perhaps curtains and valances for beds, made of a kind of cloth named for Kidderminster in Worcestershire, where it was first woven.

one pair of Blankets twenty pair of Stockings and divers other Goods now ready to be produced in Court.

And Since his Arrival here he hath not given to the Govr: nor Such other Person or Officer as was appoynted to receive the Same a true & perfect Inventory or Invoyce of the Lading of the sd Ship as by the sd Act is Enjoyned and directed.

Whereby the sd Goods and Ship with all her Guns Amunition Tackle Furniture and Apparel becomes Lost & Forfeited as in the sd Act is directed one third part to his Majty his heirs and Successrs: one third part to his Excy: the Governr: and the other third part to the Informer for which he humbly prays Decree of this Honble: Court for Condemnation accordingly.

John Taylor Advocate
Dionisius Wright[32]

To which the defendant John Hamelton Master of the sd Ship Providence appeared and by his Council put in the following Answer.

Virga: ss
Cur: Adm: July 12th. 1699

Gowin Corbyn &c: agst John Hamelton Master of the Ship Providence &c:

And the sd John Hamelton doth Say That the sd Libel of Complaynt Exhibited agst him the sd John he ought not to be Compelled to Answer in the Court of Admiralty for that by the Clause of the Act of Parliament whereon the Libel is grounded It is directed That all offences against the sd Clause Shall be Prosecuted in any of his Majtyes Courts in Such of the sd Lands Islands Plantations Colonyes Territoryes or Place where Such Offence was Committed And at the time of the making and Establishing the sd Act his Majty had no Such Court as this Court of Admiralty Established in this Colony the Place where the sd Offence is Supposed to be done and committed therefore he prayes that he may not be any further put to Answer the Libel of the sd Corbyn Exhibited agst him in this Court of Admiralty.

B Harrison pro defendant[33]

Which sd Answer being a Plea to the Jurisdiction of this Court on Arguing thereof the Same was over Ruled for that this Court hath full Power and Conusance[34] of the sd Complaynt or Information and therefore the sd Plea Adjudged Insufficiant and directed that a further and other Answer be put in to the sd Libel of Complaynt which was accordingly done in these Words (Vizt).

---

[32] Dionisius Wright, an immigrant from England about 1671, was evidently a resident of James City County. It is said that he was a trained lawyer; he was helping Taylor to prosecute in the case.

[33] Defendant's counsel was probably Benjamin Harrison, clerk of the General Assembly, later acting attorney general and advocate of the Court of Vice-Admiralty.

[34] A variant form of *cognizance*, in legal usage until modern times.

Virga: ss
Cur: Adm: July 12th. 1699

Gowin Corbyn &c: agst John Hamelton Master of the Ship Providence of Dublyn &c:

And the sd John Hamelton Saving & reserving to himself all future Advantages & Exceptions as well to the Libel of the Complaynant as to his many other Errors and incerteyntyes in the Process by him taken for Answer doth Say That he is not Guilty of the breach of the sd Statute or Act of Parliament in the manner & Form as is Expressed and Set forth in the sd Libel and this he is ready to Veryfye as the Court Shall direct &c:

B Harrison pro defendant

Then the Court Adjourn'd 'till to morrow morning ten a Clock

Thursday July 13th. 1699

The Court being Sat and having fully heard the Evidences and Examinations upon Oath of Seven Persons as well for our sd Sovereign Lord the King his Excy: the Govr: and the Informer as the sd John Hamelton Master of the sd Ship Providence for the further Consideration thereof Adjourn'd 'till to morrow morning Nine a Clock.

Friday July 14th. 1699

Att which time being Sat and having fully Considered the Proofs and Allegations on both Sides And it appearing by the Oath of John Moor a Saylor on Board the sd Ship Providence That when at Sea off of the banks of New Found Land he had knowledge of Some goods on Board the sd Ship the Cask being staved in the Hold in which the sd Goods were in As also by the Oath of Catherine Murrel a Servant Passenger on Board the sd Ship that She likewise Saw at Sea Goods which was packt up in Ruggs which was Say'd to be taken out of a Cask that was Staved in the Hold and belonging to Mr: Cromwel and that after Arrival in the Bay[35] upon Sight of a Sloop Comeing towards them two pair of Blankets was Sent for out of the Hold and put upon Cabyns As also by the Oath of Robert Mongomery one other Saylor belonging to the sd Ship That at Sea off of the banks of New found-Land he came to the Knowledge of goods being on Board the sd Ship the Cask in which they were in being Staved in the Hold of the Ship and that upon their comeing into the Bay upon Sight & Approach of a Sloop the goods which he had Seen in the Hold was by the Masters Order Sent for up out of the Hold and by his Order & direction by him and others Stowed and put away in Cabyns particularly Curtins and a Red Coat like those (if not the very Same) Shewed in Court and that he with three other Seamen particularly the aforesd John Moor carryed the sd goods in Cask on Shoar by the Order of the sd Master and delivered them to Mr: William Woodbridge[36] and the sd John Moor likewise declaring that he was in the Boat

[35] The Chesapeake Bay.

[36] This was perhaps William Woodbridge of Farnham Parish in Richmond County, on the north side of the Rappahannock River and to the northwest of Middlesex County.

Carrying two Cask a Shoar to the sd Woodbridges (tho he knows not what was in them) And it further appearing by the Oath of Mr: William Woodbridge that he had recd Several Letters from one Andrew Cromwel of Dublyn particularly by the sd Ship Providence wherein was conteyned an Invoyce of goods that he had recd Several Goods which were mentioned in that Invoyce which he beleives might come in the sd Ship Providence and was brought to his House by Some of the Seamen belonging to the sd Ship & that they were like if not the Same Shown in Court as Curtins and Vallians a Red Coat Stockings blankets flynts Nayls Powder knives Forkes Ink horns fish hooks Wash balls horn Combs blew Shirts white Shirts and Ruggs As also by the Oath of Fergus MackLaughlin Servant Passenger on Board the sd Ship that he knew of Several Goods on Board the sd Ship by the Staving of the Cask that they were pack't in That upon Arrival in the Bay and on Sight of a Sloops approaching towards them which they tooke to be a Man of Warr Sloop the Master and Merchants Consulted what Should be done with the sd Goods whether they Should be thrown overboard or how disposed off at last it was agreed that they Should be Secured by being pack't under Cabyns which he assisted in doing that he remembers green Curtins & brown Curtins which he beleives to be the Same Shown in Court That he Saw a Letter directed to Mr: William Woodbridge which was Say'd to concern the sd goods that he found a Letter in the Cabyn Sign'd Andrew Cromwel which was directed to Mr: Ewin the late Master of the sd Ship (which sd Letter was produced in Court) and wherin directions is given for the disposing of the sd goods and that he had kept the sd Letter ever Since in his own Possession untill he delivered the Same to the Kings Advocate As also by the Oath of Mr: Corbyn Griffyn[37] that he was with the Informer Gowin Corbyn at the House of Mr: William Woodbridge when he Seized Several Goods which was the Same or very like those Shown in Court that the sd Woodbridge Acknowledged that they came from and belonged to Andrew Cromwel of Dublyn And it appearing that one Andrew Cromwel was comeing over in the sd Ship Providence from Dublyn but being taken Ill upon the sd Ships puting into King Sale[38] went on Shoar And for that the aforesd goods are of the Growth Production & Manufacture of Europe and no Certificates or Cocquets being produced that the sd goods were Shipped in the Kingdom of England Wales or the Town of Berwick and for that the sd Master hath not according to the sd Act of Parliament delivered to his Excy: the Govr: or Such other Person or Officer by him thereunto Authorized and appoynted a true Inventory or Invoyce of the sd goods but hath unladen and put on Shoar the sd goods without any Such account given (as appears by his Entry under his hand produced in Court and by him acknowledged to be his hand) It is therefore Considered Adjudged & Decreed and the Sentance of the Court is That the sd Ship Providence with all her Guns Amunition Tackle Furniture and Apparel and the sd Seven Sets of Kedderminster Curtins and Vallians one pair of blankets and twenty pair of Stockings be[39] Lost and forfeited and devided according to the sd Act of Parlament one third

[37] Corbin Griffin, of Middlesex County, was Gawin Corbin's nephew.
[38] Kinsale, a port in County Cork, southeast Ireland.
[39] From this point the manuscript is in a different hand.

thereof to our Sovereigne Lord the King one third thereof to his Excy: the Govr: and the other third to the Informer.

Edw: Hill

A true Coppy
Miles Cary Regr:

From which sd Judgment and Decree the sd Defendant John Hamelton Master of the sd Shipp Providence prayes he may be Admitted to Appeal to the high Court of Admiralty in England to have a rehearing of the Premises before that high and Honble Court whereupon it is considered and the sd Shipp Providence with all her gunns Tackle Apparrell Ammunition and furniture with the sd seven Setts of Kederminster Curtins and Vallions one pr Blanketts and Twenty pr Stockins as aforesd are Ordered to be Valued and Appraised by Sufficient men upon their Oaths and Mr Thomas Loyd Mr David Gwin[40] Capt Richard Smith Commander of the Benjamin & Mary of London Capt Robert Ross Commander of the Dublin Merchant and Capt George Simson Commander of the Ship Globe of Liverpoole or any three or more of them are Authorised and Appoynted to Value and Appraise the sd Ship with all her Guns Tackle ammunition furniture and Apparrell and the sd seven setts of Kederminster Curtaines & Valions one pr of Blanketts and twenty pr of Stockins as aforesd they being first sworne before Capt Wm Mosely Mr James Baughan and Mr Francis Gouldman Justices of the Peace for Essex County[41] or any one of them and that the sd Appraisemt be returnd to the Register of the Court of Admiralty at James City on Tuesday the first day of August next for further proceedings to be had thereon.

Thursday August 3th 1699

The Court being Satt and the Appraisement of the sd. Shipp Providence &c being return'd into Court and the Defendant John Hamelton Master of the sd Ship Appearing time is given for the payment of the sd Appraisement in ready money or by good and Sufficient bills of Exchange.

which sd Appraismt is as followeth Vizt:

Virga ss

In Obedience to the within writt Wee the Subscribers did Accordingly meet the 20th of July 1699 on board the ship Providence of Dublin and being Sworne by Mr James Baughan did Appraise the sd Shipp and all her Appurtenances as Allso a Certain parcell of goods Exhibited by Gowin Corbin Esqr at Hobbs hole as followeth Vizt

---

40 Thomas Lloyd and David Gwynn were justices of the peace for Richmond County.

41 Essex County is on the south side of the Rappahannock River, northwest of Middlesex County. Hobb's Hole, now called Tappahannock, was a port town in Essex County, to which the *Providence* had probably been taken.

Hull Masts and Standing Riging			£150:00:00
1500 Weight of old runing riging 8/ per Ct			006:—:—
Pump and Blocks			005:—:—
1500 Weight of Cables 9 in about at 15/ per Ct			011:05:—
½ a hauser 5 in about 300 weight att 10/ per Ct			001:10:—
500 Weight of Junk at 2/6 per Ct			000:12:06
4 old Patararoes[42] att 5/			1:00:00
1 Suite of Sayles qtt[43] 500 yds at 4d per yd			008:06:08
2 Iron potts spitt & Hearth			001:05:00
3 Anchors 2000 Weight att 20/			020:00:—
			204:19:02
20 pr Stockins at 7/ per doz	00:11:08	}	
7 Setts of Curtaines & Vall 14/	04:18: 0	}	005:15:08
1 pr Blankets	00:06: 0	}	
			£210:14:10

Thomas Loyd Seal
David Gwin Seal
Richd Smith Seal
Robert Ross Seal

Monday October the 9th 1699

The Court being Sat and the Defendant John Hamelton Master of the sd Shipp Providence having time to this day for payment of the sd Sum of £204:19:02 the Appraisement of the sd Shipp According to the condition of the Appeal prayed for in ready money or by Sufficient bills of Exchange and having faild in the performance thereof therefore the Condemnation of the sd shipp Providence with all her Gunns Amunition Tackle furniture & Apparell and the sd seven Sets of Kederminster Curtains & Vallians one pr Blanketts & twenty of Stockins is Confirm'd as aforesd.

Edw: Hill

A true Copy
Miles Cary Regr:

While the business of the *Providence* was still not concluded, on August 9, 1699, Hill represented to the governor on behalf of the officers of the Court of Vice-Admiralty that they had had more than their usual trouble and expense in going to Middlesex County to try the *Providence.* They had thus saved the inconvenience and costs of bringing the witnesses to Jamestown, the usual place for holding the vice-admiralty court, and they asked to be compensated from money paid for the ship. Hill tendered an account

[42] *Patararo* is a variant of *pedrero,* a small piece of ordnance.
[43] The abbreviation for *quantity* may be *qy.*

of charges for the prosecution. From the appraised value of ship and cargo, the judge was to have a fee of seven percent, or £14.16.0, and each of the other three officers of the court was to have a fee of three percent, or £6.6.6; for extraordinary trouble and expenses, there was an allowance of £5.4.0 to the judge and of £3.13.6 to each other officer. The attorney general was to have a fee of £5, with an allowance of £2 for extraordinary trouble and expenses. The Council ordered payment of the total sum of £57 sterling according to Hill's account.[44]

On October 29, William Byrd, auditor of Virginia, was instructed by the Council to empower Ralph Wormeley, secretary of Virginia, Robert Carter, naval officer for the district of Rappahannock River, and Gawin Corbin, or any two of them, to sell the *Providence,* then lying in the Rappahannock River, by auction or otherwise and at such time and place as they saw fit. However, nearly six months later the ship was still not sold, for William Byrd reported to the governor and Council on April 16, 1700, that a Mr. Eccles had offered to buy the ship for £100 sterling in bills of exchange, with Ralph Wormeley and Gawin Corbin as securities. The Council instructed Byrd to sell the ship to Eccles at the price he offered, if no one would give more.[45]

There is no further news of the *Providence* until May 23, 1700, when the Council considered Gawin Corbin's complaint to the governor that the judge and other officers of the Court of Vice–Admiralty had received unusually large fees and charges upon the condemnation of the *Providence* (and thus decreased the amount of Corbin's share). The Council declared the fees and charges very reasonable and ordered them to be paid. Finally, on September 4, the Council journal noted that Governor Nicholson had decided to give up his third share of the proceeds from the *Providence,* to be used for "the Makeing and prepareing landings at the two ports of the City of Williamsburgh."[46]

The first case known to have been tried in the Virginia Court of Vice–Admiralty in 1700 was that of the ship *Jane* of Dublin.[47] At some time in

---

[44] *EJC,* II, 7-8.

[45] *EJC,* II, 20, 60.

[46] *EJC,* II, 75, 107. The two ports were at College Landing on Archer's Hope Creek, south of Williamsburg, and at Capitol Landing on Queen's Creek, northeast of Williamsburg.

[47] Late in February of 1699/1700 two men were alleged to have been brought into Virginia, by sea, without payment of duties; they were seized and the attorney general was ordered to proceed upon the seizure. There being no further mention of the matter, it is not possible to say whether there was a prosecution, or in what court, but regardless of the marine aspect of the case, the offense would probably have been regarded as one against a Virginia act, and not tried in the Court of Vice–Admiralty. *EJC,* II, 42-43.

February 1699/1700, as the record of the trial suggests, Peter Hack, deputy collector for the lower district of Potomac River, seized the *Jane* as an illegal trader, and the attorney general was instructed to prosecute on behalf of the King.

When William Thornton, master of the *Jane,* asked for a speedy trial, one was ordered for March 16. The trial was not held then because one of the most important witnesses was in Maryland. On March 18, however, in order that the ship should not risk damage, or the ruin of her voyage even if she were acquitted, the governor directed Richard Lee, naval officer and collector for the lower district of Potomac River, Robert Carter, Richard Chichester, collector for the district of Rappahannock River, and Peter Hack, or any two of them, to have the ship appraised. Then, if Thornton could give security to answer for the value of the ship, she should be discharged, and Thornton might go about his business as if the seizure had not been made; but if he could not procure the security, the seizure was to stand until Thornton came to trial.[48]

No evidence of an appraisal has been found. If it was made, one must suppose that Thornton did not offer the security required, for the trial was held, at last, on April 20 and 22, 1700:[49]

Virga: ss
Att the Court of Admiralty hell'd at James City the 20th day of April in the twelfth year of the Reign of our Sovereign Lord William the third King of England Scotland France and Ireland Defender of the Faith &c: Annoq Dom 1700.
Before the Honble: Edward Hill Esqr Judge of the sd Court
Appear'd William Thornton Master of the Ship Jane of Dublyn and Exhibited the following petition in these Words

Virga: ss
To his Excy: Francis Nicholson Esqr his Majtyes Lieut: and Governr: Genll: of Virginia
William Thornton Master of the Ship Jane of Dublyn
Humbly Sheweth
That about two Moneths Since the sd Ship was Seized by Mr: Peter Hack Deputy Collector of the lower part of Potomock River on pretence of her not being a Legall Trader whereupon your petitioner pray'd for a Speedy Tryal which accordingly was Ordered But the sd Hack having nothing to Charge the sd Ship with would not then Exhibit any Information against her pretending they were in want of

48 *EJC*, II, 45.

49 The proceedings are in C.O.5/1311 ff. 125-128. Governor Nicholson sent them to the Council of Trade and Plantations with his letter of June 10, 1700.

an Evidence from Maryland and therefore would put off the Tryal till the time of this Genll: Court.[50]

But as yet the sd Hack or any other Person hath not Exhibited any Information agst the sd Ship nor can yr petitioner be Informed when he will So that your petitioner is in danger of being a greater Sufferer without any Prosecution then he could otherwise have been if the sd Ship had been Condemn'd and at last it is to be feared She will be utterly lost for the Worm[51] is just now comeing on So that her bottom will be eaten out and the petitioner having her Loading of Tobacco by him which he cannot take Freight for in another Ship Least at last his own Ship Should goe home Empty and So he will be ruined that way and if he lets the Loading Lye by him and a Speedy Tryal of the sd Ship be not Ordered then he is likely both to loose the Ship by the Worm and have his Tobacco much damnyfyed by lyeing all the year in the Country besides the Loss of the Market.

Therefore your petitioner humbly prayes that Some Directions may be given in the premises either that the sd Ship may be Speedyly Tryed or not that he may order his Affairs accordingly being Necessitated if the sd Tryal be longer deferred to Ship his Effects in other Ships and for himself to goe away and leave her his Men being already Several of them gon and the rest resolved to goe at the Petitioners return to them if the Ship be not brought to her Tryal.

Aprill 17th. 1700 [52]

By his Excy: in Councill

This Petition is referred to the Honble: Edward Hill Esqr Judge of the Court of Admiralty for him to Order a Speedy Tryal of the Ship therein mentioned according to the petitioners prayer.

By his Excyes: Command
B Harrison

Whereupon the Court demanded of the sd Peter Hack (mentioned in the sd petition) being present in Court what he had to Alleage agst the sd Ship who Declared that he had Seized the sd Ship Jane of Dublyn (being within his District) upon the Information of Mr: Richard Chichester his Majtyes Collector for the District of Rappahannock River and Mr: John Hay of Middlesex County as an Illegal Trader that he had Assurances under their hands they would make good their sd Information But that of his own Knowledge he had nothing to alleadge against the sd Ship.

---

50 The spring session of the General Court in 1700 was supposed to open on April 15, and continue for eighteen days, Sundays excluded. The session was held, and presumably at the appointed time. *EJC,* II, 55.

51 The shipworm, or teredo, is not a worm, but a marine bivalve mollusk, whose two shells have surfaces adapted for boring into wood, on particles of which the shipworm feeds. It did great damage to wooden ships.

52 This date stands between the petition above it and the order in Council beneath it, in such a position that it may belong to either. A reasonable conjecture is that Thornton offered his petition when the General Court began its session on April 15, the governor in Council referring it to Edward Hill on April 17. Although the executive journal of the Council has no record of a meeting on April 17, the governor could have arranged an impromptu (and unrecorded) meeting of the councillors then sitting as judges in the General Court.

Then it was demanded of the Advocate if he had any thing to alleadge against the sd Ship who answered that he had nothing of his own Knowledge nor had recd any Information from the sd Collector or Informers whereupon to ground a Libel of Complaynt but was ready to Prosecute any Information that Should be given him by any Person whatsoever but none Such appearing he had nothing to offer therein.

Then it was further demanded of the sd Thornton [if] he had any thing to Justyfye himself a Legal Trader whereupon he produced the following Register and Certificates the Register is in these Words

Port Dublyn

Jurat Robert McKerrel that the Ship Jane of Dublyn whereof William Thornton is at present Master now Bound for Virga: being round Stern'd of one hundred Tons or thereabouts was Built near Shoreham in Kent in England about the year one thousand Six hundred Eighty Five and that the sd Robert McKerrel John Eccles Andrew Brice & Thomas Kirkpatrick all of this City Merchants are at Present Owners thereof and that no Forreigner directly or Indirectly hath any Share or part or Interest therein Dated this twenty Second day of July Sixteen hundred Ninety Eight.

Jurat Coram Nobis — Robert McKerrell
Martin Tucker Collr: — Wm. Alcock D Compt.
Seal — Seal

The Certificates are in these Words

Port Bewmares[53]

These are to Certyfye all whom it doth Concerne That Security is given to the Chief Officers of his Majtyes Customs in the Port of Bewmaris concerning the Ship or Vessel called the Jane of Dublyn Burthen one hundred Tons or thereabouts whereof William Thornton is Master Mounted with one Gun Navigated with Eleaven Men Pink Built and Bound for Virga: an English Plantation In America with Several Goods Wares or Merchandizes with Condition that if the sd Ship or Vessel Shall Load any Sugar Tobacco Cotton Wooll Indico Ginger Fustick or other Dyeing Wood of the Growth Production or Manufacture of any English Plantation in America Asia or Africa the Same Commodytyes Shall be by the sd Ship or Vessel brought to Some Port of England Wales or to the Port or Town of Berwick upon Tweed and be there unloaden and put on Shoar the danger of the Seas only Excepted Dated at the Custom–House Bewmaris the Seventh day of June in the Eleaventh year of the Reign of our Sovereign Lord William King of England &c: Ann: Dom: 1699.

Wm: Lewis Collr:
Seal[54] — Seal[54]
Rand Evans — Griffith Parry
Dept: Cust: — D Compt:

---

[53] Beaumaris is a port town on the east side of the island of Anglesey in Wales, across the Irish Sea from Dublin.

[54] The word *Seal,* the signature, and the title are in the margin, beside the text of the register.

Signed by us the Commrs: of his Majtyes Customs at the Custome House London 14 June 1699

Ben: Overton C Godolphin Walter Yonge Robt: Henly

Port Bewmaris

These are to Certyfye all whom it doth Concern That the twenty Ninth day of May 1699 came before us the Chief Officers of his Majtyes Customs in the Port of Bewmaris William Thornton Master or Commander of the Ship or Vessel Called the Jane of Dublyn Burthen one hundred Tons or thereabouts Mounted with one Gun Navigated with Eleaven Men and two Boyes Built English and produced a Certificate and made Oath That at Potomack in Virga: he became Bound to his Majtyes use on or about the twenty fourth day of March last with Condition That all Such Sugar Tobacco Cotton Wooll Indico Ginger Fustick or other Dyeing Wood of the Growth Production or Manufacture of any English Plantation in America Asia [or] Africa as Should be Loaden on Board the sd Ship or Vessel at any of the sd English Plantations Should be brought to Some Port of England Wales or Town of Berwick upon Tweed and be there Unloaden and put on Shoar the danger of the Seas only Excepted And it is hereby further Certyfyed that there hath been discharged and Landed out of the sd Ship or Vessel within the aforesd Port of Bewmaris one hundred Sixty Seven hhds of Tobacco in Cask and Eighteen thousand five hundred Ninety Nine pound in Bulk for which his Majtyes Dutyes have been here Satisfyed and payd Dated at the Custome–House on the Ninth day of June in the Eleaventh year of the Reign of our Sovereign Lord William King of England &c: Annoq Dom: 1699.

Wm: Lewis Collr:

Seal [55]
Rand Evans
D Cust:

Seal [55]
Griffith Parry
D Compt:

Sign'd by the Commrs: of his Majtyes Customs at the Custome–House in London the fourteenth day of June 1699

Ben: Overton C Godolphin Walter Yonge Robt: Henly

And prayed that the sd Ship might be discharged from the sd Seizure.

Then the Court Adjourn'd till Monday Morning Seven a Clock.

Monday Aprill the 22d 1700

The Court being Sat and having duly Considered the premises And for that the sd Register and Certificates as afore sd appears to be fayre & good and Pursuant to the Several Acts of Trade and Navigation And no Cause or Suspition of their being Counterfeit Appearing in them It is therefore Considered Ordered and Decreed And the Sentence of the Court is That the sd Ship Jane of Dublyn be discharged from the sd Seizure.

Edw: Hill

[55] The word *Seal,* the signature, and the title are in the margin, beside the text of the certificate.

A true Copy
Miles Cary Regr:

Exactly one week after the *Jane* of Dublin was discharged, Captain William Passenger in H.M.S. *Shoreham* found a pirate vessel, *La Paix,* or *Peace,* at the southern end of the Chesapeake Bay and captured her after a battle that went on for about ten hours. The battle, the trial of the pirate vessel, and the tangled consequences provide one of the most spectacular events of the period, especially as they are illuminated by an uncommon abundance of related documents, including two copies of the proceedings at the trial, one that Passenger sent to the Admiralty, and this copy sent by Nicholson to the Council of Trade and Plantations:[56]

Virga: ss
Att the Court of Admiralty helld at Hampton Town[57] on Saturday the Eleaventh day of May in the twelfth year of the Reign of our Sovereign Lord William the third of England Scotland France and Ireland King Defender of the Faith &c: Annoq Dom 1700.
Before the Honble: Edward Hill Esqr Judge of the sd Court
Came Capt: William Passenger Commander of his Majtyes Ship the Shoram[58] and Exhibited the following Libel in these Words

Virga: ss
May the 11th: in the 12th year of his Majtyes Reign Annoq Dom: 1700.
To the Honble: Court of Admiralty
William Passenger Commander of his Majtyes Ship the Shoram as well for and in behalf of his Majty: as for and in behalf of himself Officers and Company on Board the sd Ship[59]
Humbly Gives this Court to Understand and be Informed That on the 29th

---

[56] The proceedings printed here are in C.O.5/1311 ff. 41-48, sent with Nicholson's letter of June 10, 1700, to the Council of Trade and Plantations. The other copy, sent by Captain Passenger to the Admiralty, is in Adm.1/2277 unnumbered pages.

[57] Hampton is at the end of the peninsula between the York and James rivers. It was close to a good anchorage, and easy to reach by land or water from the capital, still at Jamestown.

[58] The *Shoreham* had arrived in Virginia on April 10, 1700, to patrol the coast and protect shipping. She was a ship of the fifth rate, with 28 guns and a crew of about 110 men. Passenger to Admiralty, April 13, and June 11, 1700, Adm.1/2277 unnumbered pages; J. Burchett to W. Popple, March 29, 1700, C.O.323/3 ff. 143-144.

[59] The proceeds of a prize ship were regularly divided among its captors, it appears, with the Crown and Admiralty at times receiving shares. Uncertainty about dividing the proceeds was not unknown. On May 7, 1700, Governor Nicholson informed Captain Passenger "that if any part of the Prize belonged to Him as Governour being on board in the fight, he would not make any pretentions thereto, but did freely give to him (the said Capt Passenger)." And in April 1702, Passenger asked the Admiralty to advise him how to distribute the proceeds from the *Peace,* as he did not know how to set about the distribution. *EJC,* II, 71; Passenger to Admiralty, April 20, 1702, Adm.1/2277 unnumbered pages.

day of Aprill last past in his Majtyes sd Ship the Shoram within the Cape of Virga:[60] Hee Ingaged Faught & tooke a Company of Pyrats or Sea Robbers which were in a Ship Called the Peace of about 200 Tuns Burthen Mounted with 20 Guns which sd Company of Pyrats or Sea Robbers in the aforesd Ship for Several days before their being Soe taken did in an Open Warlike Hostile and Pyratical manner Assault Attack Fight take Rob Burne & Spoyle Several Merchant Ships belonging to the Subjects of our Sovereign Lord the King (Vizt)

A Pinke Call'd the Baltimore John Loveday Master

A Sloop Call'd the George Joseph Forrest Master

A Ship Call'd the Pensylvania Merchant Samuel Harrison Master

A Ship Call'd the Indyan King Edward Whitaker Master

A Ship Call'd the Nicholson Robert Lurting Master

Who in a Peaceable and Lawfull manner were Comeing into and goeing out of the aforesd Cape of Virga: with their Several Goods & Merchandizes &c: And also the aforesd Company of Pyrats or Sea Robbers in the aforesd Ship at & upon the aforesd time and Place in a Hostile and Warlike manner Did Fight against Oppose Resist and Endeavour to take his Majtyes sd Ship the Shoram but they being Overcome & taken as aforesd the aforesd William Passenger in behalf as aforesd prayes Condemnation of the aforesd Pyrats Ship Called the Peace with all her Guns Ammunition Tackle Furniture and Apparel to be divided and proportioned according to the Rules and Orders of the Sea in Such Cases made and Provided &c:

W Passenger

Then Mr: Advocate Exhibited a List of Evidences desiring that they might be Examined and Testyfye their Several Knowledges Relating to the Spoyles and Depredations made by the sd Pyrats and of their being taken as aforesd by answering to Several Interrogatoryes which Interrogatoryes are in these Words

First where were you Born; to what Prince are you Subject how long have you been So and where is your Usual Place of Residence.

2dly Doe you Know the Ship Concerning which you are now Examined Called the Peace were you present when She was taken Was she a Ship of Warr, or a Private Man of Warr or a Privateer or a Pyrat who was She taken from at what time what Built is She off and what Burthen by what Ship or Vessel was She taken who were Commanders of the Ship that tooke her how many Guns had She what Resistance did She make against the Ship that tooke her how many Men had She on Board her belonging to her and of what Nation were they what Prisoners had they on Board the sd Ship and of what Nation Were they and where and when were they taken.

3dly What doe you Know of the sd Ship and her Mens Commiting any Pyracy

[60] Passenger's account of his fight with the pirate ship (sent by Nicholson to the Council of Trade and Plantations) is in C.O.5/1311 ff. 29-30. The engagement took place to the west of the Capes, Cape Charles to the north and Cape Henry to the south, and specifically in Lynnhaven Bay, at the southern end of Chesapeake Bay in what is now the City of Virginia Beach.

Robbery or Spoyl on the High Seas or any other Place against his Majtyes Subjects or any others.

4thly Doe you Know whether the Bulk of the sd Ship hath been broken Since her being taken or that any of the Tackle Furniture Goods Wares Merchandizes Provisions Jewels Plate Mony or any other thing whatsoever which Were in the sd Ship at the time of her being taken hath been by the Commander Officers or Company of the Ship that tooke her or by any other Person whatsoever taken out Carried away Concealed or any Way Imbezeled.

5thly Whether during the Chace of the sd Ship Soe taken or before She was taken were not Some of the Peices of Ordnance or any other Goods Wares or Merchandizes or other things thrown Over Board.

Then Capt: John Aldred Commander of his Majtyes Ship Essex Prize[61] was Called and Sworn and to the first Interrogatory Answer'd

That he was Born in England A Subject to the Crown of England and Resident in London.

To the Second Interrogatory

That he was on Board his Majtyes Ship the Shoram when the sd Ship Called the Peace was taken by Capt: William Passenger Commander of the sd Shoram[62] that She was taken on Monday the 29th of Aprill last past in Lyn Haven Bay from a Company of Pyrats beleives her to be Dutch Built about two hundred Tons Mounted with twenty Guns made Resistance by firing great Guns and Small Shott from an hour by [Sunn?] [63] in the morning to three a Clock in the afternoon being about ten hours about an hundred & Sixty men belonging to her the greatest part of them French Men with Some Dutch and English and about Forty or fifty English Prisoners on Board.

To the Third

Negativeley as to his own Knowledge.

To the Fourth

Negativeley.

To the Fifth

Negativeley.

Then Allexander Wedgeberry & Benjamin Spanter Seamen belonging to his

---

[61] The *Essex* prize, a ship of the sixth rate with a crew of 60, and mounting 14 or 16 guns, arrived in Virginia on March 27, 1698. She was put to flight by a pirate ship of much greater strength on July 26, 1699, in Lynnhaven Bay; on August 4 the Council advised Nicholson to ask the King for a ship of sufficient strength to defend the colony against pirates. From about mid–April until early in May of 1700, the *Essex* was being careened and refitted in the Elizabeth River, across the Chesapeake Bay and south of Hampton. J. Burchett to W. Popple, December 15, 1698, C.O.323/2 ff. 417-419; Aldred to Admiralty, March 28, 1698, Adm.1/1435 unnumbered pages; *EJC*, II, 4-5, 59; C.O.5/1311 f. 80.

[62] Passenger's account of the engagement notes that Governor Nicholson, Captain Aldred, and Peter Heyman came on board the *Shoreham* around 10 o'clock on the evening of April 28, while the ship was at anchor about three leagues from the pirate ship.

[63] The word in brackets is indecipherable in the copy of the proceedings that Nicholson sent to England, and is supplied from the copy Passenger sent, though the spelling is not clear even there. If the word is *Sunn,* the phrase *from an hour by Sunn* presumably means "from a time when the sun had risen," for on April 29, sunrise was at 5 o'clock.

Majtyes sd Ship Essex Prize was Called and Sworn and to the first Interrogatory answerd

That they were Born in England Subjects to the Crown of England and Resident in England

To the Second

That they were on Board his Majtyes Ship the Shoreham when the sd Ship Called the Peace was taken by Capt: William Passenger Commander of the sd Shoreham that She was taken on Monday the 29th of Aprill last past from a Company of Pyrats Dutch Built two hundred tons 20 Guns made Resistance by firing great Guns & Small Shott about ten hours about one hundred and fifty or 160 men belonging to her most French Men & about forty English Prisoners on Board.

To the third

Negativeley.

To the Fourth

Negativeley.

To the Fifth

Negativeley.

Then Thomas Murry Samuel Harrison Joseph Wood and John Lympany were Called and Sworn and to the first Interrogatory answer'd

That they were all Natives of England Subjects to the Crown of England and that they the sd Murry Harrison & Wood were Residents in Pensylvania and the sd Lympany in England.

To the Second

That they all Knew the Ship Called the Peace being Prisoners on Board the sd Ship when She was taken by Capt: William Passenger Commandr: of his Majtyes Ship the Shoreham within the Capes of Virginia on Monday the 29th of Aprill last past that they declared them selves to be Pyrats[64] that they beleive her to be Dutch Built of 200 Tons 20 Guns and about 150 men belonged to her that She Resisted for about ten hours by fireing great Guns & Small Shott the Pyrats Generally French with Some Dutch and English that they had on Board about forty or fifty English Prisoners of which they were part being taken in the Pensylvania Merchant of which the sd Samuel Harrison was Commander the 24th day of Aprill last past.

To the third

That they were taken in the Ship Pensylvania Merchant bound from London to Philadelphia in the Latitude of 37 degr: odd minutes in Soundings after a Nights Chace and firing of Several Guns they came up with them Commanding them to Strike and the Master Samuel Harrison to Come on Board they stript all the Seamen and passengers to the Number of thirty one persons and after part of two days plundering and pillaging they Burnt the sd ship (being the 25th day of Aprill) and Stood in 'till they made the Land and then came to an Anchor and the next day Stood for the Capes of Virga: declaring their intentions of Watering and Meeting a Pink that belonged to them came in Sight of two Ships whereupon they

---

[64] The pirates declared themselves to be pirates.

the sd Prisoners were Commanded into the Hould of the sd Ship Soon after which it appeared that they had taken the Ship Indyan King Edward Whitaker Master and the Friendship of Belfast and comeing into the Capes of Virga: Saw two Ships at an Anchor one of which by their Assaulting and firing of Guns they tooke being the Nicholson Capt: Robert Lurting Commandr: the other makeing his Escape and as they Suppose into James River[65] then they came to an Anchor in Lyn Haven Bay having under their Command three Ships and a Sloop then they went a Plundering the sd Ships and Carried to the Side of the sd Ship Nicholson the Sayles belonging to the Indyan King that they Saw Several hhds of Tobacco thrown out of the sd Nicholson and floating in the Bay and to make room in their own Ship to Stow what they had Plundered threw out of their sd Ship Several Bolts of Canvis peices of Oanibrigs[66] and other course Linen which they had taken from our sd Ship the Pensylvania Merchant and Employ'd themselves most part of Sunday Night in removing Provisions from the sd Sloop to their sd Ship and the sd Nicholson 'till near Seven a Clock on Monday morning at which time a Ship being very near which came out of James River the Capt: of the Pyrat Commanded us down into the hold of the Ship Saying it was a Man of Warr Soon after She was ingag'd with the sd Ship 'till about four a Clock in the afternoon which sd Ship was his Majtyes Ship Shoreham Commanded by Capt Wm: Passenger In the Ingagement the Pyrats Ship was forced a ground and they thereby in a dispairing Condition Seeing no hopes of Escaping So that they resolved with them selves to blow up their sd Ship having been at their (pretended) Devotion in Order thereto but by us the Deponents and the rest of the Prisoners on Board being Endeavourd (for our Self preservation) to be perswaded from it one of the Deponants John Lympany undertook and after much intreaty was by them the Pyrats Permitted to Swim on Board his Majtyes sd Ship the Shoreham to make Known their Deplorable Condition and Resolution of the sd Pyrats and finding his Excy: the Govr: on Board his Majtyes sd Ship did in the behalf of the sd Prisoners humbly Supplicate his Excy: that Capitulations might be granted the sd Pyrats that the sd Prisoners might be preserved from present Destruction which was So far Granted that the sd Pyrats Surrendred themselves and the sd Prisoners deliver'd from their Captivity.[67]

To the fourth Interrogatory

Capt: Samll: Harryson Answers That he Saw the Boates belonging to his Majtyes Ship the Shoreham pass and Repass from the sd Pyrats Ship on Board the sd Shoreham with Plunder but what it was he Knows not and likewise that Several other Boates besides those belonging to the sd Shoreham was on Board the sd Prize a Plundering.

---

[65] This was the merchant ship that brought the report of a pirate ship in Lynnhaven Bay to Hampton, where Passenger heard the report on April 28.

[66] The word is hard to decipher, but the other copy of the proceedings has *Osinbrigs* or *Osnibrigs,* a variant of *osnaburgs,* the coarse linen cloth named for Osnabrück in Germany, where it was originally made.

[67] Nicholson sent a copy of the terms of capitulation, dated April 29, between 4 and 5 p.m., to the Council of Trade and Plantations, and he conveyed the terms to the Virginia Council on May 7, 1700. C.O.5/1311 ff. 29-30; *EJC,* II, 70.

And the sd Joseph Wood declares that he Saw in the Capt: of the Pyrats[68] Chest that Stood in the Cabyn Several peices of Stuff Kenting[69] and Lace & other Linnen about three or four hats with other Small things a Gilded box with four or five Watches particularly a Watch Enamell'd with green and Red belonging to one of the Deponants Thomas Murry which was in Mr: Manwarings hands.[70]

And the sd Thomas Murry Declares that he came on Board his Majtyes sd Ship Shoreham with the Capt: of the Pyrat that the next day he Saw the Shorehams Boat comeing from on Board the Pyrat on Board their own Ship with two Boxes Mark't CxR as also Writing Paper Powder and Flints.

To the Fifth

They Answer that they were in the Hold of the Pyrats Ship and Knows Nothing.

And then the Court Adjourn'd 'till Monday Morning Eight a Clock.

Monday May the 13th. 1700

The Court being Sat Joseph Man was Called and Sworn and to the first Interrogatorry answer'd

That he was Born in England a Subject to the Crown of England and his Chiefest place of Residence here in Virginia.[71]

To the Second

That he Knowes the Pyrats Ship being on Board his Majtyes Ship the Shoram in attendance on his Excy: the Governr: when She was taken that She was a Pyrat Fighting agst the Kings Colours and taken from[72] Such on Monday the 29th of Aprill last past That he has no Judgement in Ships Built or Burthen that She was taken by Capt: William Passenger in his Majtyes sd Ship Shoreham and Reputed to have twenty Guns mounted that She made a Vigorous Resistance from Six a Clock in the Forenoon 'till three in the afternoon by Firing great Guns and Small Shott that he was Standing by Peter Heyman Esqr when he was Wounded and Kill'd that he Saw part of another mans Skull the Body being thrown over Board[73] that they were about 150 Men chiefly French with Some Dutch and English and that there was on Board about forty or fifty English Prisoners.

To the Third

Hee Knowes Nothing of his own Knowledge.

To the Fourth

Negativeley as Knowing Nothing.

---

68 The pirate captain was called Lewis (or Louis) Guitar (or Guittar). *EJC*, II, 82.

69 Kenting is a kind of fine linen cloth, perhaps named for the English county of Kent.

70 Manwaring was an officer belonging to the *Shoreham.*

71 Joseph Man, in a deposition taken for the trial of some of the pirates from the *Peace,* deposed that he was at Hampton when Captain Aldred came ashore and told Governor Nicholson and Captain Passenger, in Man's hearing, about being aboard a pink that had escaped from a pirate in Lynnhaven Bay. Man is probably the person who had served as a courier to the government of Maryland around June–November 1698, towards the end of Nicholson's tenure as governor there. C.O.5/1311 ff. 61-62; *Md. Arch.* XXII, 171, 175, 176, 233, 234, 235, XXIII, 432, 523.

72 The other copy of the proceedings also has *taken from,* although the sense calls for *taken as.*

73 Passenger informed the Admiralty that aside from Heyman, four men of the *Shoreham* were killed in the fight, and six were wounded, two of whom died later. Passenger to Admiralty, May 3, 1700, Adm.1/2277 unnumbered pages.

To the Fifth

Negatively.

Then Joseph Forest & Edward Whitaker was Called and did not appear.[74]

Then Robert Lurting was Called & Sworn.

And to the first Interrogatory Answer'd That he was Born in England a Subject to the Crown of England and Resident in London.

To the Second

That he Knowes the Pyrats Ship being on Board the sd Ship when She was taken that She was a Pyrat and taken as a Pyrat by Capt: William Passenger in his Majtyes Ship the Shoram on Monday the 29th of Aprill last past that She is Dutch Built two hundred tons Burthen & twenty Guns mounted that She resisted by firing great Guns and Small Shott from Six in the forenoon 'till four in the Afternoon and by their own relation one hundred and fifty men in Company That they were generally French but of most Nations they Reckoned fifty odd English Prisoners of which he was one being taken in the Ship Nicholson within the Capes of Virga: on Sunday the 28th of Aprill last past.

To the third

That he Knowes that the sd Pyrat tooke the sd Ship Nicholson whereof he was Commander that they kept the sd Ship in Possession bringing him on Board the sd Pyrat that they threw over Board out of the sd Ship Nicholson above one hundred hogsheds of Tobacco besides Bulk Tobacco Plundering the Ship and Striping both Seamen and Passengers.

To the Fourth

That he Knowes Nothing of the Bulk of the sd Pyrats Ship being Broken.

To the Fifth

That he Knowes great quantityes of Goods were thrown over Board out of the Prize Seeing them Floating in the Bay as he was Carryed from his own Ship on Board the sd Pyrat that Sayles was brought by the Pyrats on Board his sd Ship which was afterwards Claymed by the Commander of the Indyan King and Deliverd accordingly as also twelve Small barrels which he beleives to be Flower for that one of them which is open & in Spending is Flower.

Then it was demanded of Mr: Advocate if he had any other Evidences to Examine who Answered that he had Several more but Mr: Attorney Genll: Moveing in the behalf of Capt: William Passenger that the Evidences already produced and Examined were Sufficient and therefore (for Saving the Courts time) Prayed the Court Would proceed to their Decree and that the sd Ship with all her Guns &c: according to the Inventory produced might be Condemned &c: which sd Inventory is as followeth

An Inventory of the Ship Lapey Pyrat taken by his Majtyes Ship Shoreham on the 29th day of Aprill 1700 Capt: William Passenger Commandr:

A Ship Eighty four foot by the Keel twenty five foot by the Beam and Eleaven foot deep in the Hold with one Deck Flush Fore and Aft An half deck to the Mayn Mast and a Fore Castle twenty Iron Guns mounted Carriages and all other

[74] These were the masters of the *George* and the *Indian King,* both taken by the *Peace.*

things belonging to them Eight Guns and Carriages in the Hold Five Guns more in the Hold.

Masts

Mayn Fore and Mizon Mast and Bolt Sprit

Top Masts

Mayn Fore Mizon and Sprit Sayl topmasts

Yards

Mayn Fore Mizon Sprit Sayl yards

Mayn Fore Mizon and Sprit Sayl Top Sayl yards

one Cross Jack yard

Sayls

Mayn Fore Mizon and Sprit Sayles a Sprit Sayl

top Sayl and Mayn Stay Sayl

Shrouds

Mayn Fore and Mizon Shrouds

Mayn Fore Mizon & Sprit Sayl top mast Shrouds

Stayes

Mayn Fore and Mizon Stayes

Runing Riging for the Bolt Sprit

2 Sprit Sayl braces

2 pennants for the braces 2 Sprit Sayl Clue Cones

2 Sprit Sayl Sheets 2 Standing Lifts 2 runing Lifts

1 hawse for the Bolt Sprit

Sprit Sayl

Top Sayl Riging 2 braces 2 pennants for the braces

2 Lifts 2 Clue Cones 1 Crane Cone

Runing Riging for the Fore Mast

Jeers one 2 Lifts 2 braces

2 Cluegarnets 2 tacks 2 Sheets 2 hawses 2 buntlines

1 [Beasline?] [75] 2 bowlines a parrel and Rope

Runing Riging for the Mayn Mast

Jeers one 2 tacks 2 Sheets 2 hawses

for the yard one Punt Line 2 Mayn bow lines and bridles 1 Cluegarnet 1 brace 1 pendant

Mizon Runing Riging

Jeers one 4 brailes a parrel & Rope

The rest of the Runing Riging all on Board but Shot to peices 2 top tackles 1 forefould tackle 2 tackles for the Tiller one Anchor and one Cable New one Anchor & Cable left in Lyn Haven Bay Reported to be taken up by Capt Lurting 2 Stoppers for the Anchors, 1 Shank painter 2 Pumps Speers brakes and boxes 2 Spare upper boxes 3 lower boxes one Watch glass one Compass 3 half hourglasses 2 barrels of Tarr and Pitch one grin stone trough Axeltree & Winch besides abundance of more

[75] This appears to be the word in Passenger's copy of the proceedings. It is illegible in Nicholson's copy.

Lumber on Board 2 Stoppers at the Mayn Mast one dog Stoppers with other Stoppers on the deck for the Cables.

W Passenger
Robt: Desbrough
Wm: Robinson[76]

Bread 13 Cask—Flower 19 barrels two barrels of Musty gave the hogs—one Cask of Grout half full one Cask of Oat meal—one barrel of Biefe Powder in half barrels and quarter barlls. 32 Fire Arms 30—Pistoll Shott barrels 2 Paper Royal Ream one Match half a hundred Weight Boxes of Candles 4—Canvis in parcels 4 Jarrs of Oyl 3

And then the Court Adjournd 'till tuesday morning Seven a Clock

Tuesday May 14th. 1700

The Court Met and Adjourn'd 'till Wednesday Morning Seven a Clock

Wednesday May 15th. 1700

The Court being Sat and having Consider'd the Premises have thereon Ordered Adjudg'd & Decreed and the Sentance of the Court is That the sd Ship Called the Peace as aforesd be Forfeited with all her Guns Amunition Tackle Furniture & Apparel to be divided and proportioned according to the Rules and Orders of the Sea in Such Cases made and Provided.

Edw: Hill

A true Copy
Miles Cary Regr:

After the trial of the *Peace* ensued various other pieces of business arising from the capture and condemnation of the pirate vessel. The most important business, to the authorities in Virginia as well as in England, was the disposition of the captured pirates, not a matter in the cognizance of the Virginia Court of Vice-Admiralty, and only partially a concern of the colony. Three pirates were tried, condemned, and executed in Virginia; eight others had died in Virginia of unspecified causes; the remainder, about a hundred of them, were sent to England.[77]

Towards the end of May the governor and Council began to give orders

[76] Robert Desbrough was lieutenant of the *Shoreham* and William Robinson was the master. Passenger to Admiralty, June 23, 1701, Adm.1/2277 unnumbered pages.

[77] The three pirates tried and executed in Virginia were not covered by the terms of surrender: one had made his way to shore, and two were in one of the captured merchant ships when the pirate ship surrendered. The governor issued a commission for the trial of these three pirates to be held at a court of oyer and terminer on May 13, at which the pirates were condemned. (The proceedings at this trial are in C.O.5/1411 ff. 362-415.) The pirates broke out of jail after the trial but were recaptured and executed by June 10. The surviving pirates were sent to England on the fleet of merchant ships that sailed from Virginia on June 9, under

for the disposal of the stores and effects taken on the *Peace*. An order of May 23 instructed Passenger to have the provisions appraised and distributed among the merchant ships that were to carry the pirates to England, while masters of those ships were to have such captured small arms as they needed to keep the pirate prisoners under control. Passenger was to allow the prisoners as much of the canvas and old sails taken from their ship as they required for clothing and other needs. He was authorized to take the pirate ship's guns for use on the *Shoreham,* except for six that he was to deliver to one of the King's ships lately arrived from Maryland. And, finally, he was instructed to sell the *Peace* "and all other things thereto belonging" as advantageously as he could. These "other things" did not include the goods and effects of the pirates, whatever they may have been, for on June 5 the Council ordered them to be secured and inventoried until the King's pleasure was known.[78]

Passenger arranged to sell the *Peace* on July 4, but bad weather kept any buyer away. He next proposed a sale on July 25, but clearly to no purpose, for he then took the prize to Hampton for a sale on August 20. On August 23 he informed the governor that nobody had bought the ship, and he thought it would be useless to set another sale, because every one had the notion he could not establish a good title to the ship and she could be claimed by her first owners. When the ship was still unsold on May 8, 1701, the Council advised Passenger it would be in the King's interest to load the vessel with some of the tobacco that would otherwise be left in Virginia. He followed the advice and sent the ship to England with about 200 hogsheads of tobacco, to the common benefit of the King and the Virginia growers. The final disposition of the ship has not been discovered.[79]

the escort of the *Essex*. They were evidently tried and condemned by November 11, when the Admiralty was informed of the King's pleasure that the pirates Lewis Guittar, Francis William Hubart, John Juransen and Peter Loumos, lately convicted, should be hung up in chains after their execution. *EJC,* II, 65-66, 73, 75, 84, 88; C.O.5/1311 ff. 74, 75-78; *CSPD,* XI, 144.

[78] An appraisal of the bread and flour was made, and reported on June 5 by Robert Lurting, Richard Tibbotts, William Cooper, Edward Whitaker, and John Coker. (Tibbotts, Cooper and Coker were masters of the *Ann & Mary, Jefferys,* and *Susannah,* and like Lurting and Whitaker they were in the convoy that sailed on June 9.) In their opinion, the bread was worth 20 shillings a hundred (pounds, probably), and the flour was worth 26 shillings a hundred. No other appraisal is known. Passenger informed the Admiralty he had taken four of the pirate's guns for use on the *Shoreham.* Later, he informed the Admiralty that, by Nicholson's order, he had disposed of things from the *Peace* to the value of more than £200; he had spent the proceeds on supplies for the *Shoreham* and intended to distribute the reimbursement he expected among the ship's officers and crew. *EJC,* II, 77-78, 88-89; C.O.5/1311 f. 28; Passenger to Admiralty, June 11, 1700 and April 20, 1702, Adm.1/2277 unnumbered pages.

[79] On June 19, 1701, considering Passenger's request to be excused from paying the duties on about 200 hogsheads of tobacco aboard the *Peace,* soon to sail for England, the Council decided that since the *Peace* had been taken, condemned, and registered in Virginia, and in view of Passenger's meritorious service, he should be accounted a Virginia owner and enjoy

The capture of the *Peace* must have been a disappointment to her captors in several respects. It looks as though the shares in the prize that Passenger and his crew might have looked for were diminished by the distribution of provisions, stores, arms, and guns from the *Peace,* the impounding of the pirates' effects, and the lack of any buyer for the ship. The capture of the *Peace* did lead to the seizure of the *George,* once taken by the *Peace,* as an illegal trader, but the prosecution of the *George* was a failure.

At some time in May 1700 Captain Passenger seized the Pennsylvania sloop *George,* that he had released at the end of April from capture by the pirate *Peace.* He made the seizure on the grounds that the sloop was an illegal trader, belonging to an old Spaniard aboard her; his information came from one Thomas Young, formerly belonging to the *George.*[80]

The trial of the sloop was held on June 5:[81]

Virga: ss

Att the Court of Admiralty Hell'd at the Court House of Elizabeth City County[82] on Wednesday the fifth day of June in the twelfth year of the Reign of our Sovereign Lord William the third by the Grace of God of England Scotland France and Ireland King Defender of the Faith &c: Annoq. Dom: 1700.

Before the Honble: Edward Hill Esqr: Judge of the sd Court.

Appeared Capt: William Passenger Commander of his Majtyes Ship the Shoreham and by his Majtyes Attorney General[83] Exhibited the following Libel of Complaynt against the Sloop George Joseph Forrest Master in these Words Vizt:

Virga: ss

Admiralty Court June 4th. 1700 In the twelfth year of his Majtyes Reign.

William Passenger Commander of his Majtyes Ship the Shoreham in the behalf of his Majty his Excellency and himself doth Libel and Set forth to this Honble: Court

1 That by one Act of Parliament made in the Seventh and Eighth years of the

---

the privileges of such. This meant that he was exempt from the payment of various duties, including that of 2 shillings on each hogshead of tobacco exported from the colony, in accordance with acts of the General Assembly of March 1661/2 and October 1669. See Hening, II, 133–134, 135–136, 272.

80 Passenger reported the seizure in a letter of May 20, 1700, probably to Governor Nicholson, abstracted in *CSPC,* XVIII, 317. The letter is not in C.O.5/1311, as it should be, and must have been misplaced when the Board of Trade Papers were recatalogued about 1910. One wonders whether the Thomas Young named as Passenger's informant could have been the John Young who testified in the trial of the *George,* as a former member of her crew.

81 The proceedings are in C.O.5/1312 Part I ff. 63-65, sent to the Council of Trade and Plantations with Nicholson's letter of August 27, 1700.

82 Elizabeth City County, of which Hampton was the county seat, lay at the tip of the peninsula between the James and York rivers. The county became extinct in 1952, when it was incorporated in the present City of Hampton.

83 The attorney general was perhaps acting in place of the advocate, who had written on June 1 to excuse his failure to attend the court. *EJC,* II, 89.

Reign of his Present Majty Entituled An Act for Preventing Frauds and Regulating Abuses in the Plantation Trade[84] It is Enacted in these Words "That after the five and twentyeth day of March 1698 No Goods or Merchandizes whatsoever Shall be Imported into or Exported out of any Colony or Plantation to his Majty in Asia Africa or America belonging or in his Possession or which may hereafter belong unto or be in the Possession of his Majty his heirs and Successrs: or Shall be Laden in or Carried from any Port or Place in the sd Colonyes or Plantations to any other Port or Place in the Same the Kingdom of Engld Dominion of Wales or Town of Berwick upon Tweed in any Ship or Bottom but what is or shall be of the Built of Engld or of the Built of Ireland or the sd Colonyes or Plantations and wholly own'd by the People thereof [or any of them, and navigated with the Masters] and three fourths of the Mariners of the sd Places only &c: under payn of forfeiture of Ship and Goods one third part whereof to be to the use of his Majty his heirs and Successrs: one third part to the Governr: of the sd Colonyes or Plantations and the other third part to the Person who Shall Informe and Sue for the Same by Bill Playnt or Information in any of his Majtyes Courts of Record at Westminster or in any Court in his Majtyes Plantations where Such offence Shall be Committed."

2 That Joseph Forrest Master of the Sloop George Some time in the Moneth of May in the twelfth year of his Majtyes Reign did Import in the sd Sloop George into the County of Elizabeth–City Several Goods and Merchandizes that is to Say four Cask of Bisket one hundred barrels of Meal and twenty hhds of Strong Beer which sd Sloop is not wholly Own'd by the People of England Ireland or of any of his Majtyes Colonyes or Plantations but is part Own'd by one John Corse a Forreigner.

3 Therefore the sd Sloop George and all her Goods are Forfeited one third part to his Majty one third part to the Govr: and the other third part to the sd William Passenger Informer.

Wherefore the sd William Passenger Prayes Condemnation and a Decree thereof accordingly.

Barth: Fowler Attor: Genll:

To which the defendant Appear'd and by his Council put in the following Answer

June 5th. 1700

And the sd Joseph Forrest Sayth That the sd Sloop is wholly Own'd by the

[84] The act was 7 & 8 William III, c. 22. *Statutes*, III, 609-614. The quotation is from section 2. The words in brackets, omitted in the manuscript, are supplied from the printed act. The &c a few words farther on marks the omission of this statement of excepted vessels: "(except such Ships only as are or shall be taken as Prize, and Condemnation thereof made in one of the Courts of Admiralty in England, Ireland, or the said Colonies or Plantations, to be navigated by the Master and three Fourths of the Mariners English, or of the said Plantations as aforesaid, and whereof the Property doth belong to English Men; and also except for the Space of three Years, such foreign-built Ships as shall be employed by the Commissioners of his Majesty's Navy for the time being, or upon Contract with them, in bringing only Masts, Timber and other naval Stores for the King's Service from his Majesty's Colonies or Plantations to this Kingdom, to be navigated as aforesaid, and whereof the Property doth belong to English men)."

People of England Ireland or of his Majtyes Colonyes or Plantations and that no part thereof is Owned by the sd John Corse or any other Forreigner and therefore he prayes to be dismist &c:

B Harrison pro Defendant

Then Mr: Attorney desired the following Evidences might be Called to Wit John Young who Appeared and was Sworn and Declared

That he Knowes the Sloop George being a Mariner belonging to her when She was taken by the Pyrats that the sd John Corse the Spanyard Declared to the French Pyrats that the sd Sloop George Belonged to him and Should goe no more to Phyladelphia.

That he Knew Adrian Scroop mentioned in the Register to be one of the Owners of the sd Sloope That he Own'd he had the Sixtyeth part of her for which he pay'd Seven pounds And that he the sd Scroop Own'd himself to be a Pyrat That the Deponant belonged to the John & Susannah of Bristoll and left the Service of the sd Ship & Entred himself on Board the sd Sloop.

Then John James Mate of the sd Sloop was Called and upon the Motion of the Complaynant was Sworn who Declare'd

That he Knowes the Sloop George that She was Built at Burlington in West Jersey by Peter Resnier that the sd John Corse was Concern'd in the Building of her that he Built her for one Hunt in Barbados that he had Spoke to him to goe Master of her that he heard She was afterwards Sold to Charles Saunders of Phyladelphia that he Knows not that the sd Corse has any part or Interest in her that the sd Sloop was Seized at Phyladelphia as belonging to the sd Corse and upon Tryal acquitted.[85]

That the sd Sloop was Publickly Sold by Ince[86] of Candle and Bought by one Mr: Douglass and as he heard for the sd Joseph Forrest the General discourse before the sd Sale being that the sd Douglass was to buy her for the sd Forrest.

Then Samuel Jones Marriner on Board the sd Sloop was Called and Sworn for the Complaynant

Who Declared That he Knew the Sloop George being a Mariner on Board her that he Knew her at Phyladelphia before She was Masted And that he Knowes of No Owner of the sd Sloop but the sd Joseph Forrest.

Then the Defendant produced the following Register in these Words

Pensylvania

I Adrian Scroop of the City of London Mariner Doe Swear That the Sloop George of Phyladelphia in the Province of Pensylvania whereof Joseph Forrest is at present Master being a Square Stern'd Sloop Burthen about twenty five Tons was Built at Burlington in the Province of West New Jersey in the year one

---

[85] No record of the trial has been found.

[86] This should be *Inch.* A sale by inch of candle was a sale by auction, in which bids were accepted as long as a small piece of candle burned, with the last bid made before the candle went out securing whatever was being bid for. Another version has it that the sale went on until a candle burned down to a mark on it.

thousand Six Hundred Ninety & Eight And that I the sd Adrian Scroop and the sd Joseph Forrest are at present Sole Owners thereof And that No Forreigner directly nor indirectly hath any Share or part or Interest therein

Adrian Scroop

Seal
Wm: Penn Pr: Gr:[87]

These are to Certyfye all whom it may Concern That the above Named Adrian Scroop did upon the day of the date of these presents at Phyladelphia aforesd make Oath in manner & Form as is above mentioned before me the Collector of his Majtyes Customs for the sd Port of Phyladelphia who Administred the Same the Proprietary and Governr: of the sd Province being present according as by an Act made Septimo et Octavo Gulielmi Tertij Angliae &c Regis is required In witness whereof I have hereunto Set my hand and Seal of Office this 21st day of March in the 12th year of the Reign of William the third of England &c: King Annoq Domini 1699/1700

Seal
Jno: Bewley
Collr:[88]

Then Edward Johns was Called for the defendant and Sworn

Who Declared That he was Present and Saw the sd Joseph Forrest Pay a Sum of Mony to Isaac Norris in part of Payment for the sd Sloop but knowes not the Just quantity thereof.

Then the Defendant further Produced the sd Peter Resnier Builder of the sd Sloop his Sale of the sd Sloop to Charles Saunders & Edward Hunt The sd Charles Saunders Sale to Isaac Norris And the sd Isaac Norris Sale to him the sd Jos: Forrest.

Upon all which premises it is Consider'd And for that the sd Sloop is duly Registred according to the sd Act of Parliament made in the 7th & 8th years of his present Majtyes Reign for Preventing Frauds and Regulating Abuses in the Plantation Trade And no Sufficient Proof Appearing that the Property of the sd Sloop is Alter'd by any part of her belonging to the sd Corse or any other Forreigner It is therefore Consider'd Adjudg'd and Decree'd And the Sentance of the Court is That the sd Sloop George be Dismist from the sd Seizure and Prosecution.

Edw: Hill

A true Copy
Miles Cary Register

---

[87] The word *Seal,* the name, and the title are in the margin beside the text of the register.
[88] The word *Seal,* the name, and the title are in the margin beside the text of the certificate.

On receiving Passenger's letter of July 6, 1700, in which he reported his seizure of another sloop (this one from Maryland) as an illegal trader, the Council at its meeting on July 9 ordered the attorney general to inform the judge of the Court of Vice–Admiralty about the seizure, so that he might set a trial.[89]

The trial took place on July 23 and 24, with the result that the sloop was condemned as not properly registered:[90]

Virga: ss
Att the Court of Admiralty held at James City on Tuseday the 23d: day of July In the twelfth Year of the Reign of Our Sovereign Lord William the 3d: by the Grace of God of England Scotland France And Ireland King Defendr: of the faith &c Annoque Dommini 1700

Before the Honble: Edward Hill Esqr Judge of the sd Court

Appeared Bartholomew Fowler Esqr: his Majties. Attorney Genll: And Exhibited the following Libel Against the Sloop the Slowfeild George Slaycomb Master In these Words

Virga: ss
To the Honble. his Majtyes: Court of Admiralty

William Passengr: Commandr: of his majesties Ship the Shoram as well for And in behalf of his majesty And for And in behalf of his Excellency Francis Nicholson Esqr his majties: Lieut: And Governr: Genll. of Virga as for And in behalf of himself doth Libel And Set forth.

That by one Act of Parliament made Anno Regni Gulielmi 3d Regis Angliae Scotiae Franciae & Hiberniae Septimo et Octavo Entituled (An Act for preventing Frauds And Regulateing Abuses in the Plantation trade) It is by one Clause[91] thereof Enacted And that from And After the five & twentieth Day of March which Shall be in the year of Our Lord one thousand Six hundred ninety Eight No Ship or Vessell whatsoever Shall be Deemed or Pass as a Ship of the Built of England Ireland wales Berwick Guernsey Jersey or of Any of his Majties Plantations in America So as to be quallified to trade to from or in Any of the Said Plantations Untill the person or persons Clameing property in Such Ship or Vessell Shall Register the Same as followeth That is to Say if the Ship at the time of Such Registr: Doth belong to Any Port In Engld: Ireld: wales or to the Town of Berwick upon Tweed then proof Shall be made upon Oath of one or more of the owners of Such Ship or Vessell before the Collecto: & Comptroller of his Majties. Customs in Such Port or if at the time of Such Registr: the Ship belong to Any of his Majties Plantations In America or to the Islands of Guernsey or Jersey then the like proof to be made before the Governr: together with the Principall officer of

---

[89] *EJC*, II, 92.

[90] The proceedings are in C.O.5/1312 Part II ff. 65-68, sent to the Council of Trade and Plantations with Nicholson's letter of December 2, 1701.

[91] Section 17.

his Majties: Revenue Resideing in Such Plantation or Island which Oath the sd. Govrs: & Officers of the Customs respectively are hereby Authorized to Administr: in the tenour Following Vizt: Jurat A B that the Ship [name] of [Port] whereof [Masters Name] is at present Master being a [kind of Built] of [Burthen] tuns was Built at [place where] in the year [time when] and that [owners name] and [ ] of &c[92] are at Present owners thereof And that no Foreigner Directly or Indirectly hath Any Share or Part or Intrest therein &[93] which Oath being Attested by the Govr: or Custom House officer Respectively who Administred the Same undr: their hands And Seals Shall After haveing been Registred by them be Delivered to the Master of the Ship for the Security of her navigation a Duplicate of wch Register Shall be Imediately transmitted to the Commrs of his Majties. Customs In the Port of London in ordr: to be Entred in a Genll: Registr: to be there Kept for this purpose with Penalty upon any Ship or Vessel tradeing to from or in Any of his Majties Plantations in America After the sd: five And twentieth day of March And not haveing made proof of her built And Property as is here Directed that She Shall be Liable And She is hereby made Liable to Such Prosecution And forfeiture as Any Foreign Ship Except Prizes Condemnd in the high Court of Admiralty would for tradeing with these Plantations by this Law be Lyable to. And that by Another Clause[94] of the sd: Act it is Also Enacted that After the five & twentyeth Day of March one thousand Six hundred ninety Eight no goods or Merchandizes Whatsoever Shall be Imported into or Exported out of Any Colony or Plantation to his Majesty: In Asia Africa or America belonging or in his Possession or which may hereafter belong unto or be in the Possession of his majesty his heires or Successors or Shall be Laden in or Carried from Any one port or place in the sd: Colonyes or Plantations to Any other Port or place in the Same the Kingdom of Engld: Dominion of wales or town of Berwick upon Tweed in Any Ship or Bottom but what is or Shall be of the Built of England or of the Built of Ireland or the sd: Colonyes or Plantations And Wholly ownd by the People thereof or Any of them And navigated wth: the master And three fourths [of the Mariners][95] of the sd: Places only[96] &c. undr: payn of Forfeiture of Ship And goods one third part whereof to be to the Use of his Majesty his heirs And Successors: one third part to the Governr of the sd: Colonyes or Plantations And the other third part to the person who Shall Inform And Sue for the Same by Bill playnt or Information In Any of his Majties. Courts of Record at Westminstr: or in Any Court in his Majties: Plantations Where Such offence Shall be Comitted

2 That George Slaycomb Marriner Mastr: of the Sloop Called the Slowfeild Some time in the month of July in the 12th year of the Reign of our Sovereign

---

[92] The words in brackets are written without brackets in the manuscript, where they stand just above the spaces they occupy here. The present arrangement, including the brackets, is that of the printed act in *Statutes.* The end of the oath in the printed act is [*Owners Name*] *of* [ ] *and* [ ] *of, &c.*

[93] From this point through *Lyable to,* section 18 of the act is quoted.

[94] Section 2.

[95] Words in brackets, omitted from the manuscript, are supplied from the printed act.

[96] At this point the manuscript omits a proviso of the printed act exempting prize ships and vessels employed in the King's service, for which see note 84 above.

Lord William the third King of England Scotland France And Ireland Defender of the faith &c Did Import into Elizabeth City County in this his Majesties Colony And Dominion Severall goods And Merchandizes In the Said Sloop S[l]owfeild that is to Say one Cable a quantity of Powdr: And Shott a parsell of new Pewter five Iron Potts Some Ready made wereing Apparrell And Some House hold Stuff And other Lumbr: And hath not made proof of the Built And property of the sd Sloop or Vessel by Produceing a Registr: of the Same According to the form Set Down in the Aforesaid Act

3 Therefore the sd. Sloop Slowfeild with all her Goods is become forfeited one third part to the Use of his majesty one third part to his Excellency the Govr: And the other third part to the Informant

Wherefore he Prays Condemnation And Decree thereof Accordingly

Barth: Fowler Attorney Genll

To which sd Libel or Complaynt the Defendant George Slaycomb Appeard And by Dionisius Wright his Attorney prayed time for the Perusal And Consideration of the sd Act of Parliamt. wch. being granted After Consideration thereon the sd wright put in the Following Answr: to the Said Libel of Complaynt Vizt.

Virga: ss

And the Defendant Comes And for plea Saith that the sd. Sloop Slowfeild is not Lyable to A Capture & Condemnation by force of the Above recited Statute but manifestly Exempted from the Same And this he is Ready to Aver and of the Same prays Judgment &c

Dionisius Wright pro Defendant

And further Pleaded the following provise of the Said Statute[97] viz "Provided Also, that nothing in this Act Shall be Construed to Require the Registring Any fisher Boats, Hoyes, Lighters, Barges or Any open Boats or other Vessels (tho of English or Plantation Built) whose navigation is Confined to the Rivers or Coasts of the Same Plantations or Place where they trade respectively but only of Such of them as Cross the Seas to or from Any of the Lands Islands Places or territoryes in this Act before recited or from one Plantation to Another"

And more over that the sd. Sloop had not Crossed the Seas but only came from Merryland So that She was not within the Intent And Meaning of the Aforesd. Statute

To w[h]ich Mr: Attorney Genll. Replied that for that the sd Sloop came from the Province of Merryland to this Plantation or Dominion with Merchandizeing goods as Aforesd. not being Registred As Aforesd. was wthin the Intent And Meaning of the Said Statute & thereby forfeited &c: as Aforesaid

The Court for further Consideration to be had thereon Adjournd till tomorrow morning Seven a Clock

---

[97] Section 20.

Wednesday July the 24th 1700

The Court being Sat and haveing Considering[98] the premises And for that the Afore Recited Statute of the Seventh And Eight of his present Majesties Reign Directs that all Ships or Vessels tradeing into or from one Plantation to Another Should be Registred as Aforesd. And for that the sd. Sloop Came with Merchandizeing Goods as Aforesd. from the Province of Merryland (A distinct Governmt: from this,) into this Govrmt: without a Registr. as is thereby Required as Aforesd, It is therefore Considerd Adjudgd And Decreed And the Sentance of the Court is, That the sd: Sloop Slowfeild wth. All her tackle Apparrell & Furniture & the sd. Recited Merchandizeing goods as Aforesaid, To witt one Cable a quantity of Powdr: and Shott A parcell of new Pewter five Iron Potts Some Ready made wereing Apparrell And some houshold Stuff And other Lumbr be forfeited And Divided According to the sd. Act One third part to the Use of his majesty one third part to his Excellency the Governr: And the other third Part to the Informer

Edw: Hill

Copy
Miles Cary Register

However, George Slaycomb offered a petition to the governor and Council (evidently read on August 8), to plead ignorance as the cause of his offense, and to beg remission of the forfeiture decreed by the Court of Vice-Admiralty. The governor and Council, taking into account the poverty of the petitioner (who probably had no means of livelihood but the sloop), and the fact that the sloop, her fittings, and cargo had been sold for only £12 sterling, freely remitted and pardoned the King's share in the forfeiture. Nicholson then remitted his share, while Passenger was entreated to surrender his share, "Pursuant to his promise made by his Letter dated July 6th 1700 when he seized the sd Vessell." [99]

The last two of this series of cases in the Virginia Court of Vice-Admiralty are alike in several respects: the two ships brought to trial, the *Mary & Ann* and the *St. Peter & Anthony,* came to Virginia with parties of French Protestant refugees intending to settle in the colony; both ships were seized as illegal traders on the grounds of a violation of the act of 7 & 8 William III for preventing frauds and regulating abuses in the plantation trade, the *Mary & Ann* as being in part owned by foreigners, the *St. Peter & Anthony* as not having her master and three fourths of the mariners English; and both ships were discharged from seizure by the Court of Vice-Admiralty.

98 The clerk inserted *haveing* with a caret but neglected to change the next word to *Considered.*
99 *EJC,* II, 102-103.

The *Mary & Ann* arrived in Virginia on July 23, 1700, bringing a party of 207 French Protestant refugees led by the Marquis de la Muce and Charles de Sailly.[100] At a Council meeting on August 8, 1700, the governor produced King William's letter of March 18, 1699/1700, ordering Nicholson to provide the refugees with land for settlement in Norfolk County, and a letter of April 12, 1700 from the Council of Trade and Plantations that recommended the refugees to the governor. There being no suitable land in Norfolk County, the Council decided to settle the French at Manakin on the James River, about twenty miles above the falls where the city of Richmond is today. Then the governor laid before the Council a letter of July 29 from Captain Passenger, reporting that de Sailly and some others of the refugees owned a quarter of the *Mary & Ann*. Thereupon, the governor ordered the attorney general and the advocate to prosecute the matter "with all possible Expedition" in the Court of Vice–Admiralty.[101]

There is no record of the date when Passenger seized the *Mary & Ann*, although he informed the Admiralty he had made the seizure because de Sailly had told him he owned a quarter of the vessel.[102]

The trial began on August 21, was adjourned to September 5, and then resumed on September 25:[103]

Virga ss
Att the Court of Admiralty Held at James City[104] on Wednesday the twenty first Day of August in the twelfth Year of the Reign of Our Sovereign Lord William the third by the Grace of God of England Scotland France & Ireland King Defendr. of the faith &c Annoque Domini 1700.
Before the Honble. Edward Hill Esqr. Judge of the sd Court Appeared Barth Fowler Esqr. his majesties Attorney Genll. & in the Name & behalf of Capt William Passenger Commandr. of his Majesties Ship the Shoreham Exhibited the Following Libel of Complaynt Agst. the Ship Mary & Ann George Haws[105] Master in These Words Vizt.

---

100 A number of documents related to the earlier history of the refugee party are abstracted in *CSPC,* volumes XVII–XVIII, passim, and indexed there under the names of the French principals, the Marquis de la Muce and Charles de Sailly.

101 *EJC,* II, 101-102. The letters from the King and Council are printed in *VMHB,* XXI (1913), 181-183.

102 Passenger to Admiralty, August 29, 1700, Adm.1/2277 unnumbered pages.

103 The proceedings are in C.O.5/1312 Part II ff. 69-72, sent with Nicholson's letter of December 2, 1701, to the Council of Trade and Plantations.

104 James City, or Jamestown, was to be replaced as capital of Virginia by Williamsburg, where, according to Nicholson's proclamation of October 26, 1699, the General Assembly and General Court would be held after May 10, 1700. However, some business of the colony was still conducted at Jamestown: for example, the Council met there in executive session as late as September 7, 1700. *EJC,* II, 29, 108.

105 Passenger described Hawes as lately a lieutenant in the King's service. Passenger to Admiralty, August 29, 1700, Adm.1/2277 unnumbered pages.

Virga ss } ss
Admiralty

William Passenger Commandr. of his majesties Ship the Shoreham As well for And in behalf of his Majesty And for & in behalf of his Excy. Francis Nicholson Esqr. his majesties Lieut & Govr. Genll. of Virga As for And in behalf of himself as Informer Doth Libel & Set fourth to this Honble. Court

That by one Act of Parliamt. made Anno Septimo et Octavo Gulielmi 3d Regis Entytulled (An Act for preventing frauds And Regulateing Abuses in the Plantation trade) It is Enacted by One Clause thereof in these Words "that After the five & twentyeth Day of March one thousand Six Hundred ninety Eight no Goods or merchandizes whatsoever Shall be Imported into or Exported Out of Any Colony or Plantation to his majesty in Asia Africa or America belonging or in his Possession or which may hereafter belong Unto or be in the Possession of his Majesty his heires or Successors or Shall be Laden in or Carryed from Any One Port or Place in the sd Collonys or Plantations to Any other Port or Place In the Same the Kingdom of England Dominion of Wales or Town of Berwick Upon tweed in Any Ship or Bottom but what is or Shall be of the Built of England or of the Built of Ireland or the sd Collonys or Plantations And wholy ownd by the People thereof or Any of them & navigated wth. the Master And three forths of the Marriners of the sd places only (Except Such Ships only as Are or Shall be taken Prize & Condemnation thereof made in One of the Courts of Admiralty in England Ireland or the Said Colonys or Plantations to be navigated by the master & three fourths of the marriners English or of the said Plantations as Aforesd And whereof the Property Doth belong to English men And Also Except for the Space of three years Such fureign Built Ships As Shall be Imployed by the Commrs. of his Majesties Navy for the time being or Upon Contract With them in bringing only Masts timber And other Naval Stores for the Kings Service from his majesties Colonys or Plantations to this Kingdom to be navigated As Aforesd And whereof the Property Doth belong to English Men) Under Payn of forfeiture of Ship And Goods one third part Whereof to be to the Use of his majesty his heires & Successors one third part to the Govr. of the Said Colonys or Plantations & the other third part to the Person Whow Shall Inform And Sue for the Same by bill Playnt or Information in Any of his majestyes Courts of Record At Westminster or in Any Court in his majesties Plantations Where Such ofence Shall be Committed.

2 That George Haws Master of the Ship Mary & Ann Some time in the month of July in the twelfth year of the Reign of his present majty Did Import in the sd Ship Mary & Ann into James City County in this his majestyes Colony of Virga. in the Uper District of James River[106] Several Goods & Merchandizes to wit A Certayn quantity of Linen And Puter about the Vallue of One hundred pounds Sterl. About thirty hatts of the Vallue of twelve pounds Sterll A quantity of Books About the Vallue of two hundred pounds Sterl. And Several other Goods Wares And Merchandizes wch. sd. Ship Mary & Ann is not wholly ownd by the People

[106] James City County is bounded on three sides by the Chickahominy, James, and York rivers. The upper district of James River was the customs district.

of England Ireland or of Any his majesties Colonys or Plantations but is partly Ownd by Olivier De la Muce Charlois De Sailly Sobragen Nicoloy Peter De lom Gabriel Sturter Tertulion Sehult Peter Ferrier[107] And others of their Company who Are All Foreigners And Joyntly have the forth part of And A Share And Intrest in the sd Ship Mary & Ann Therefore the sd Ship Mary & Ann with All her Goods is forfeited one third part to his majesty one third part to his Excellency the Govr. & the other third part to the Informer.

Wherefore the Aforesd. William Passenger in the Behalf Aforesd. prays Condemnation And Decree thereof Accordingly.

Barth Fowler Att Genll

To which the Defendant George Haws per Mr. Benjamin Harrison his Councill Appeard And put in The following Answer

Virga
Admiralty } ss

George Haws Master of the Ship Mary & Ann to the Libel of William Passenger Commandr. of his majestyes Ship the Shoreham as well for And in behalf of his majesty &c for Answer Sayth

That he is Ignorant of Any Such Goods Imported into this Colony as Are mentioned in the sd Libel that he hath in noe wise offended Agst the Act of Parliament in the sd Libel mentioned for that his sd Ship is Wholly owned (as the sd Act Directeth) by the People of England Ireland or of the Plantations.

And therefore he Prays that he may be permitted without further mollestation to prosecute his Lawfull And Necessary Occasions & that he may have Reparration Awarded him for the Costs And Damages in this behalf Already Susteyned &c.

Ben: Harrison pro Respondent

Then Mr. Attorney Genll. produced three Letters from the Honble. William Byrd[108] Esqr. to his Excly the Govr. Shewing the Reasons why the Wittnesses Agst the sd Ship Mary & Ann Could not Appear before this Day &c.

And Desired the following Evidence might be Called to wit Mounsr: Charlois de Sailly who Appeard And was Sworn who haveing Declard part of his Evidence was Directed by the Court to put the Same in Writeing &c After which Mr. Attorney moved the Court that they wanted their Evidence for the King for that Marquis

---

[107] The Marquis de la Muce was correctly called Olivier, it appears, while de Sailly's name was probably Charles. Two different copies of the list of refugees (C.O.5/1312 Part I f. 31, and C.O.5/1339 ff. 3-4) give the other names here as Soubragon Nicolay, Pierre Delome (or Delomé), Gabriel Sturter, Tertulien Seheut, and Pierre Ferrier (or Terrier).

[108] William Byrd (1652-1704), member of the Council and auditor of Virginia, had been appointed by the governor and Council to assist the French refugees in their settling. He may also have had a letter recommending the refugees from his son William (1674-1744), then studying law in London. On April 10, 1700, William Popple wrote to William Byrd of Lincoln's Inn, conveying the desire of the Council of Trade and Plantations that Byrd would help the refugees with his advice, and with a letter of recommendation to his father. *EJC*, II, 101; C.O.5/1359 pp. 396-397.

De la Muce was Very Sick at the head of James River & could not Possibly Attend & prayd that the tryal might be put of till further time.

Whereupon the Defendants Councill Insisted that the tryal might be proceeded on the tryal being Begun &c: But it being Considered by the Court that the sd. Marquis Delamuce was ill & Could Not Attend & it being Alleadgd that he was a Considerable Evidence for the King was Inclinable to put of the sd. tryall whereupon the Council for the Defendant further Moving that the Wittnesses now in Court Agst. the sd. Ship Mary & Ann Might be Examined but the Same being opposd by Mr. Attorney its Referd to the time of the tryal And the sd. tryal is Referd & put of till thursday the fifth Day of September Next to be Held heer At James town And Accordingly the Court Adjourned to thursday the fifth Day of Septembr. next.

Edw: Hill

A true Copy

Test Miles Cary Regr:

Virginia ss

Att a Court of Admiralty Held at Shirley Hundred[109] on Wednesday the 25th Day of Septembr in the twelfth year of the Reign of Our Sovereign Lord William the third by the Grace of God of England Scotland France & Ireland King Defendr. of the faith &c. Annoq Dom: 1700

Before The Honble. Edward Hill Esqr. Judge of the sd Court

Whereas at a Court of Admiralty Held at James City on Wednesday the 21th Day of August Last past the tryal of the Ship Mary & Ann whereof George Haws is master is Referd till the 5th of this Instant 7ber at which time the Judge being Sick And noe Wittnesses Appearing farther time was Given for the sd tryal And the Same was Appoynted to be at this place Upon yesterday the 24th Instant And noe Evidence then Appearing but Mounsier De Sally the Court Did not Set till this Day And the sd George Haws now moving to be brought to tryal the proceedings of the Last Court in the sd Caus was Read & Monsr. Cha: De sally Examined Upon Oath whether he knew of Any Evidence to prove the matter aleagd agst the sd Ship besides himself, And why Marquis Della muce Did not Appear According to Order to which he Answered that the Marquis was Still Sick at Capt. Webbs[110] house near the falls of James River, & that he had told him Since his Sickness that

---

109 Shirley Hundred was in Charles City County on the James River, with James City County adjoining on the east. Edward Hill owned a large tract of land in Shirley Hundred, on the James River at the point where the Appomattox River joins it. The court may have sat at Shirley Hundred for the sake of Hill, who had been unwell (and died about two months later), and for the convenience of the French witnesses, the Hundred being about midway between Jamestown or Williamsburg, where the court would normally sit, and the falls of the James, near which the French were staying.

110 Webb was no doubt Captain Giles Webb of Henrico County, in which the immigrants were settled. The governor and Council somewhat later asked Giles Webb to make occasional reports on the French refugees. *EJC,* II, 131.

he remembred very little of the Matter Concerning the sd Ship &c, Onely what he had from him as the only person that was Imployed in England About her. 2dly That there is noe other person knows Anything or Can give Any Evidence in the matter noe Other ways thn he himself has Informed them.

Whereupon the Court proceeded to the tryall & Monsr Cha: De sailly Did further on his Oath Deliver his Deposission in Writeing to the Court wch was in these Words following Vizt.

After I had Seen upon the River of thems the Ship John now Mary & Ann & Spoken to a Carpenter who had repaired it Some time before wee did agree to Goe to Lumber Street[111] where it was to be Sold & to buy it if wee Could for 600 li & that I Should hold for me & partners one 4th part & Soe wee went Accordingly & haveing Spoken to A broker he promised to help us & put the Ship to 605 li Afterwards Capt. Haws did Ask me doe you Impower me to buy this Ship I Answered yea And then it was delivered to us for 605 li besides the broakers Right, After that wee went wth Capt Morely who was the owner to pay him part presently According to the Proposalls of the Sail & then not haveing money Enough Abot: me, I gave to Capt Morely ten Guineys & ten malt Ticketts[112] for Security of my fourth part till the next day that I brought him A Hundred pounds & took back my malt tickets for wch Hundred pounds Capt. Haws gave me A Receipt Undr his hand & wee went to Mr Puckly a Publick Notary About the 25th of march Last to draw the Bill of Sail & one of Releas for the 4th part to me wch. was drawn Accordingly but not Signd becaus haveing told Capt. Haws that I was A Forreigner & Could not Hold part in the Vessel, & that he Should return me my Mony, & keep the Ship for him & his freinds he sd. he would have me Concernd wth. them or Else he would not Concern himself because he would have me Imploy him Againe, & keep this Ship for the Use of our Company, & desired me to put this 4th part Undr. the name of some of our Company Naturallized Upon wch I told him wee have Severall but wee are not to be Concernd directly or Indirectly & Soe I shall be Concernd Still but he Answered it is noe matter I Shall doe well, bring me only one Naturallized & let me alone, & Soe I produced Capt Moses Jaqueau one of Our Company naturallized, & the Capt. toore the Receipt he had Given me & Gave one other to Capt. Moses Jaqueau with promise to make him A Bill of releas for the 4th part of the sd. Ship on demand And the sd. Capt: Jaqueau gave me one other Receipt that I had paid that mony out of our Common Stock & that he would not pretend to the sd 4th part Above his Shair According to his proportion & Contribution After the fraight or passage mony being paid to the sd Capt Haws the sd Jaqueau wth. me Some others Mr. Cleve & others Concernd went to pay the tradesmen after wch. the sd Jaqueau Mr Cleve & two more Signd the book & the Captens orders About the 20th of Aprill last & Mr. Cleve told us we had the Ship very cheap Since all was paid & a hundred pounds of Goods belonging to us for

[111] Lombard Street, in London near the River Thames, an important business center.

[112] Malt tickets were tickets for shares in what was called the malt lottery, promoted in 1699 by authority of Parliament, with the duty on malt as security.

the Ships Cargoe & Above a £120 more Ready mony left in banck wch. I affirm to be true the 25th. of 7ber 1700.[113]

Chars Sailly

After wch. the sd. George Haws produced a Legall Register of the sd. Ship Mary & Ann According to Act of Parliamt[114] & A Certyfycate of haveing given bond in England to return to England Wales or Berwick only Upon Consideration of all wch. & the Argument of the Kings Advocate[115] & the Defendants Councill, it is the Opinion of the Court that there doth not Appear, Suffitient Evidence to prove the Libel of Complaynt agst the sd. Ship & therefore it is Adjudged & decreed And the Sentence of the Court is that the sd. Libel be Dismist And that the sd. Ship be Dischargd from Seizure.

Edw: Hill

A true Copy

Test Miles Cary Regr:

What the governor, the attorney general, and Captain Passenger thought of the court's sentence would be interesting to know. On August 26, after he had examined de Sailly (who admitted he and others owned a quarter of the ship) and had studied de Sailly's deposition, the register of the *Mary & Ann,* and the act of Parliament concerned, the attorney general offered a formal opinion to the governor. He reviewed the facts in the case,

---

113 An earlier and slightly different version of this deposition is in C.O.5/1312 Part I ff. 53-54, sent to the Council of Trade and Plantations with Nicholson's letter of August 27, 1700. The earlier deposition is dated August 22, 1700, and signed Ch: de Sailly. It states that Captain Hawes and de Sailly saw the ship on the River Thames, then went to Lombard Street, and that they visited the notary public on April 1, to order a bill of sale and a bill of resale. In the earlier deposition, Captain Moses Jaqueau is described as living in St. Ann's Court, Soho; what Hawes promised to give Jaqueau on demand is called a bill of resale. The men who went to pay the tradesmen, de Sailly said, were "Jaqueau with me Peter Bounot [or Bouvot] Mr. Cleeve and some others"; and thereafter, Jaqueau, Cleeve, and two others signed the book and Captain Hawes's orders. In other respects the two depositions are substantially the same. The arrangement with Hawes did not work out to de Sailly's satisfaction: on August 22, 1700, de Sailly wrote a letter to Jaqueau and others in London (C.O.5/1312 Part I ff. 56-57), complaining that Hawes had treated the refugees barbarously during their voyage and let their property and provisions be stolen or destroyed. De Sailly added, without giving any details, that Hawes wished to make de Sailly and his partners lose their quarter share in the vessel.

114 There is a copy of the register in C.O.5/1312 Part I f. 62, evidently made for the attorney general. The register, dated April 10, 1700, attests that George Hawes, Alexander Cleeve, and Robert Glover, of London, are owners of the *Mary & Ann,* and that no foreigner, directly or indirectly, has any share in the vessel.

115 Presumably the advocate was assisting the attorney general with the prosecution. It may be relevant that the attorney general had asked to be relieved of his office because of his lack of knowledge and experience and his very poor health; his request was granted on September 4, 1700, although he was directed to go on with prosecution of any pending suits brought by him. *EJC,* II, 105-106.

pointed out that the register did not prove present ownership of the *Mary & Ann,* and concluded "So that upon the whole matter I am humbly of Opinion if the Matter of fact be Sufficiently prov'd that the Ship Mary & Ann and her Goods are forfeited by the Said Act of Parliament." [116]

On August 27, Nicholson wrote to the Council of Trade and Plantations, transmitting the attorney general's opinion, the deposition by de Sailly, the register of the *Mary & Ann,* with some related papers, and observed "If this Ship should not be condemned here for want of good prooff, Yet I hope she will in England; For with Submission if such Ships should escape upon the Quibles and niceties of Law, no doubt 'twould be a president for others. . . ." Nicholson went on to propose that the King's attorney and solicitor general should give their opinion on the case, since the judge and lawyers in Virginia would not pretend to have extraordinary knowledge in such cases.[117]

The governor laid before the Council on September 4 the deposition by de Sailly and other papers not identified, as well as copies of his letter of August 27, to the Council of Trade and Plantations, and his letter of August 24, to the Commissioners of Customs, not traced, but evidently on the same subject of the *Mary & Ann.* The Council of Trade and Plantations replied on December 4, expressing approval of Nicholson's dealings with the French refugees, but referred him to the Commissioners of the Customs for an answer to his comments on the case of the *Mary & Ann.* Neither Nicholson's letter to the Customs nor the reply (if there was one) has been found.[118]

About three weeks after the discharge of the *Mary & Ann,* Edward Hill, Jr., the judge's son, collector of the upper district of James River since 1699, instituted a prosecution of the *St. Peter & Anthony,* lately arrived in Virginia with a second party of Huguenots:[119]

Virga ss
Att the Court of Admiralty Held att his Majesties Colledge of William & Mary near Williams Burgh[120] on Saturday the 19th: Day of October In the twelfth Year of the Reign of Our Sovereign Lord William the third by the Grace of God of

---

[116] C.O.5/1312 Part I ff. 60-61.

[117] C.O.5/1312 Part I ff. 44-48.

[118] *EJC,* II, 105; C.O.5/1360 pp. 59-62.

[119] The proceedings are in C.O.5/1312 Part II ff. 73-79, sent with Nicholson's letter of December 2, 1701, to the Council of Trade and Plantations.

[120] The trustees and governors of the college, that stood on the western edge of the new town, had offered the use of whatever rooms in the college were required for the colony's business until the Capitol was completed. *EJC,* II, 61.

England Scotland France and Ireld King Defendr: of the faith &c Annoq: Domini 1700.

Before the Honble Edward Hill Esqr: Judge of the Said Court

John Taylor his Majties: Advocate In the name & In behalf of Edward Hill Junr: Esqr: his Majties: Collector of the Uper District of James River Exhibited the following Libel of Complaint Against the Ship St: Peter Anthony Gally[121] Daniel Perreau Master In these Words Vizt

Virga ss
Octobr:
Court of Admiralty In the 12th: year of his majties Reign Annoq: Dom: 1700

Edward Hill Junr: Esqr: his Majties: Collector of the Uper District of James River as well for And in behalf of his majesty; his Excellency the Govr: as for And In behalf of himself Humbly gives this Court to Understand And be Informed 1st: That by one Act of Parliament made Anno Septimo et Octavo Gulielmi 3d: Regis Entituled (An Act for Preventing Frauds and Regulateing Abuses in the Plantation trade) It is Enacted as Followeth

"Whereas notwithstanding Divers Acts made for the Encouragemt: of the navigation of this Kingdom And for the better Secureing And Regulateing the Plantation trade more Espetially one Act of Parliamt: made In the 12th: year of the Reign of the Late King Charles the Second Intituled An Act for Increasing of Shiping & navigation Another Act made In the fifteenth year of the Reign of his sd Late majesty Intitulled An Act for the Encouragemt: of trade Another Act made in the two & twentieth & three & twentieth years of his sd Late majestys Reign Intitulled an Act to Prevent the Planting of tobacco in England & for Regulateing the Plantation trade Another Act made in the twenty fifth year of the Reign of his sd: Late majesty Intitulled An Act for the Encouragemt: of the Green Land And East land trades And for the better Secureing the Plantation trade Great Abuses Are Dayly Committed to the Prejudice of the English navigation And the Loss of A great part of the Plantation trade to this Kingdom by the Artifice and Cuning of ill Disposed persons for Remidy whereof for the future Be it Enacted And it is hereby Enacted And Ordaynd by the Kings most Excellent Majie: by And with the Advice And Concent of the Lords Sperituall And temporall And Commons In Parliamt Assembled And by the Authority of the Same that After the five & twentieth Day of March one thousand Six hundred ninety Eight Noe goods or merchandizes whatsoever Shall be Imported Into or Exported out of Any Colony or Plantation to his majesty in Asia Africa or America belonging or in his possession or which may hereafter belong unto or be in the Possession of his majesty his heirs & Successors or Shall be Loaden in or Carried from Any one Port or place in the sd Collonyes or Plantations to Any other Port or place in the Same the Kingdom of England Dominion of wales or town of Berwick upon tweed in Any Ship or bottom but what is or Shall be of the built of England or of the Built of Ireland or the sd Colonyes or Plantations And

[121] In the proceedings, the vessel is almost always called *St. Peter Anthony*. Nevertheless, *St. Peter & Anthony* must have been the correct name.

Wholly ownd by the People thereof or Any of them & navigated wth the Master & three fourths of the Marriners of the sd: places only (Except Such Ships only as Are or Shall be taken Prize & Condemnation thereof made in one of the Courts of Admiralty in England Ireld. or the sd Colonys or Plantations to be navigated by the Master And three fourths of the marriners English or of the Said Plantations as Aforesd: And whereof the Property Doth belong to English men And Also Except for the Space of three years Such foreign built Ships as Shall be Imployed by the Commrs: of his Majties navy for the time being or upon Contract with them in bringing only Masts timber And other naval Stores for the Kings Service from his majties Colonyes or Plantations to this Kingdom to be navigated as Aforesd: And whereof the property doth belong to English men Under payn of forfeiture of Ship And goods one third part whereof to be to the Use of his majty his heires And Successors one third Part to the Govr: of the sd: Colonyes or plantations And the other third part to the person who Shall Inform or Sue for the Same by bill playnt or Information In Any of his majties Courts of Record at westminster or in Any Court In his majties Plantations where Such offence Shall be Committed.

2dly That Daniell Perreau master of the Ship st: Peter & Anthony Gally Burthen About one hundred tuns navigated with fourteen men Did Contrary to the before Recited Act, on or About the 28th Day of Septembr: Last past Import in the sd: Ship into James City County In the uper district of James River in Virga Severall goods wares And merchandizes to witt forty Six fire Lock guns[122] of the Vallue of forty pounds Sterling A percell of books of the Vallue of twenty pounds Sterling two peices of flanell qt:[123] About 40 yds. Vallue About forty Shillings a parcell of Leaden Shott of the Vallue of three pounds Sterling a parcell hatts about 2 Doz: Vallue Six pounds a parcell Shoose vallue about three pounds. fifty pounds of Powder Vallue two pounds. one ps Fustian[124] Vallue About fifteen Shillings two barrells of Iron Nayls & Axes Vallue about Six pounds Stl: one barrell of wareing Cloaths Vallue five pounds. A pair of Smiths billows, And Anvill. a percell Smiths Hammers of the Vallue of Eight pounds.

3dly That the Sd. Ship st Peter Anthony Gally is not navigated with the master And three fourths of the marriners English as by the sd: Act is Directed, And Enjoyned.

Therefore The sd Ship and Goods becomes Lost And Forfeited one third part to his majty &c one third part to his Excellency the Goveror: And the other third part to the Informr: for which he prays Decree of this Honble. Court Accordingly &c.

John Taylor Advocate

To which sd. Libell of Complaint the Defendant Daniell Perreau Master of the sd: Ship st: Peter Anthony Gally Appeard And by his Councell put in the following Answr:

---

122 These were probably flintlock muskets.

123 For *quantity*.

124 A piece of fustian, a coarse cloth of cotton and flax.

Virga ss

octobr.
Court of Admiralty in the 12th: year of the Reign of King William the third &c Annoq: Dom: 1700.

In Answer to the bill of Complaint of Edward Hill Junr: Esqr: his majties Collector: &c Daniell Perreau master of the Ship st: Peter Anthony of London Sayth that in the sd: Ship he did not Import into this Colony of Virga Any goods And merchandizes or other things whatsoever Save only the Apparrell And necessary Utencills of Certain Passengers by him brought in hither being French Refugees And the Mony to Defray the Charge of their Comeing hither being given them by the grace And favour of his most Sacred Majesty.

And the sd. Daniell Perreau further Saith that he being mastr. of the sd: Ship And four other marriners belonging to the Said Ship were Aliens Born but by Letters Patent Under the great Seal of England Are Lawfully made free Denizons of the Kingdom of England And As Such are Lawfully quallified to be master And mariners of the sd: Ship And therefore the sd: Daniell Perreau Saith that the master & three fourths of the mariners Are English as by the Act of Parliament in the sd Libell Mentioned is Directed.

B Harrison

Then Mr: Advocate Moved that the Evidences to be Examined being French men An Interpreter might be Appoynted And Sworn.

Whereupon Mr: Isaac Jamart[125] was Appoynted Interpreter And Sworn Accordingly.

Then Mr: Advocate desired Severall Evidences Might be Called And in the first place Mr: Benjamin De Joux Minister[126] who Appeard And was Sworn, And to the following Questions made the following Answers

Question Do you Know of Any goods (not yor. own) Imported In the Ship st: Peter Anthony Gally

Answer Knows not of Any goods but what was the Passengers Cloathing Utencills &c

what was Those

Axes Guns hammers Nayls Saws tools for working in the Earth And other Utencills bought by the men of the mony given them for their Passage to Virginia

Do you Know what numbr. of Guns were Imported

About forty Seaven Guns

Did they belong to the Common Stock

They were distributed Amongst those that had no Guns

where were they distributed

---

[125] Isaac Jamart is not further identified. He may have been a French immigrant, but he is not in the lists of passengers on the *Mary & Ann* (see note 107 above), or the *St. Peter & Anthony*. C.O 5/1312 Part II ff. 13 11. He was probably the man who was appointed by the Court of Vice-Admiralty to appraise a prize ship in 1706. *EJC*, III, 88.

[126] De Joux, a passenger on the *St. Peter & Anthony*, was minister at Manakin for a few years.

They were distributed In London but for fear of Imbezelment taken into his possession & distributed again here in Virga

Was there Any books besides yor own

None as he Knows of but wt: belongd to him

Do you Remembr: Any other things Imported

Flanell & blue Shirts for the Passengers which was distributed Amongst them

Was there Any Shott

four hundred pound of Shott And fifty pounds of powdr: part thereof Distributed in London & in the Ship to the passengers

Was there Any Hatts

Thirty two Hatts which were Distributed In England & on Board Save Seaven or Eight which were So bad that none of the passengers would have them

Was ther not a ps of Fustian

There was a ps of Fustian Cut into peices And Distributed but Afterwards Sown together Again

what quantity of Nayls & Axes

Knows not the quantity but there was two Small Cask tho not Enough for their Use

was there Any wearing Cloaths

There was old wearing Cloaths belonging to A woman Passenger which he beleives to be in A barrell

was there Any Smiths billows & Hammer

There was a Billows And Anvill belonging to a Smith a passenger with other Smiths tools

Do you Know the Vallue of the before mentioned Goods

The Vallue of the goods brought for the passengers About Eighty or Ninety pounds at the most

Then at the Defendants Desire the following questions were Demanded of the sd: Mr De Joux

what numbr: of Persons Able to bare Arms were Imported

About Eighty

How many Passengers were there in all

one hundred fifty five[127]

Then John Martyn[128] one of the passengers was Called And Sworn.

Do you Know of Any goods imported in the Ship st: Peter Anthony gally

yes goods belonging to the Passengers

what goods were they

Nayls hammers Guns old Shoes 400 lb Leaden Shot and bullet 50 lb: powder Some flanell wch: was cut into ps: Hatts not Very good Billows & Smiths tools belonging to A Smith the ministers books a Little blue Lining[129] to Make Shirts he had one Ready made A Small percell of Fustian Cut into peices.

---

[127] The list cited in note 125 above gives 169 passengers, with notes by Daniel Perreau setting the number at 170, and (in a confusing account of fares he charged for the passengers) at 155.

[128] He appears as Jean Martain in the passenger list.

[129] Linen, probably.

How many hatts
Knows not the quantity
How many Guns
forty Seaven
Whether there was not more Guns then forty Seaven
Some few more belonging to particuler men but Knows not how many
Then the following questions were demanded (by the defendant) of the sd: Martyn
How many men Capable of useing Guns
About Eighty
How many passengers
one hundred fifty five
Then the Complainants demanded whether the hoes nayls Guns & Axes were brought on Board Ship in Cask or by particuler persons & So put together.
He himself Carried a Gun wch: was one of the forty Seaven & About two thousand nayls on Board.
Whether the nayls & Axes were not together & Landed here in Cask.
To which the Minister & Martyn Answered that they were brought a Shoar In Barrells.
Then the Minister was Asked whether the Said Nayls And Axes were to be divided at the place of Settlement who Answerd that part was divided at Jamestown & the Rest to be divided at the Settlemt:
Then Michael Derry Cheif mate of the sd Ship was Calld & Sworn & demanded
What Goods were Put on Board the sd: Ship st. Peter Anthony & Imported here into Virga
Chests and trunks but Knows not what was in them as Also three or four Barrells
Whether Anything Else besides Chests trunks & Barrells
A pr: of Billows & An Anvill
Then Matthew Ardwyes the boat Swayn was Called And Sworn & Asked
What Goods were Imported in the sd: Ship st: Peter Anthony & put on Shoar here In Virga
He Answers that he Came on board the Said Ship when Shee was Ready to Sail And did not Know wt: was in the sd: Ship but that there was Landed at James town Beding Chests Barrells & Cloaths belonging to the Passengers as Also a pair of Billows And in Answr: Concerning the Guns that there was Long Cases.
Then the Defendants Councill Argued
That the goods Imported were the necessary utencills of the Passengers who being French Refugees Came by the Kings grace And favour to Settle here in Virga, that the Guns were not only for their defence but for to Releive them with Provisions The Books for the use of the minister nayls for building Axes & hoes for tilling the Earth And the Cloaths for to Keep them warm And All these being guifts of Charity Could not be said to be merchandizing Goods And the Master & two more french men Seamen being denizons they were navigated According to the Act of Parliamt & that they were duly quallified produced the following Instruments

I Nicholas Hayward Notary & tabellion[130] Publick dwelling In London Admitted & Sworn do hereby Certifye & Attest unto All whome it may Concern that I have Seen & perused certain Letters Patents of Denization Granted by Our Sovereign Lord King James the Second undr: the broad Seal of England dated the fifteenth day of Aprill in the 3d: year of his Said Majties Reign wherein Amongst others is Incerted the name of Daniell Perreau who thô born beyond Seas is made his Majties Leige Subject And to be held reputed And taken as a Subject Born in this Kingdom of England and may as Such purchase buy Sell And dispose of Lands tenaments And hereditaments in this Kingdom or any other of his Majties dominions as freely Peaceably & Intirely as Any Subject born in this Kingdom And that the sd: Daniell Perreau by Virtue of the sd: Letters Patents is to pay Custom And Dutyes for his goods & merchandizes only as natives do And ought to do And to Enjoy all Libertyes priviledges & franchises of a Subject born in this Kingdom without Any disturbance Impediment or molestation as by the sd: Patent Relation being thereunto had may more at Learge Appeare of All which Act being required of me the sd: notary I have granted these presents to Serve and Avail the sd: Daniell Perreau In time And place Convenient London the 27th: of Aprill Anno Dom 1687.

Seal [131]
In Testimonium Veritatis Segno meo manuali Solito Signavi & Tabellionatus mei Sigillum Apposui rogatus.[132]

Nich Hayward No[tari]us Pub[lic]us
1687

I Henry Smith Notary & tabellion Publick Admitted And Sworn do hereby Certifye And Attest Unto All whome it may Concern that I have Seen & Perused Certain Letters Patents of Denization Granted by Our Sovereign Lord King William the third undr: the broad Seal of England Dated the 29th: of Septembr: in the tenth year of his majesties Reign wherein Among others is Incerted the name of Michael Derrier who though Born beyond Seas is made his Majties: Leige Subject And to be held Reputed And taken as a Subject born in this Kingdom of England And may as Such purchase buy Sell and dispose of Lands tenaments and Heriditaments In this Kingdom or Any other of his Majties. Dominions as freely peaceably & Intirely as Any Subject born in this Kingdom And that the sd Michael Derrier by Virtue of the sd: Letters Patents is to Injoy All Libertyes Priviledges And franchizes of a Subject Born in this Kingdom without Any Disturbance Impediment or Molestation as Also permitting the Persons in the Said Patents Mentioned to be Marriners or Masters of Ships as by the sd: Patents Relation being thereunto had may more at Large Appear of all which Act being required of me the sd: Notary I have Granted these presents to Serve And Avail the sd: Michael Derrier in time And place Convenient London the 12th: of Octobr: 1698 And in the tenth year of his majesties Reign.

130 A tabellion was a variety of notary or scrivener.
131 The word *Seal* is in the margin, beside the text of the certificate.
132 In free translation, this attestation reads "In witness whereof I have signed with my usual signature and added my seal of office."

Seal [133]
In testimonium Veritatis Signo meo manuali Solito Signavi & tabellionatus mei Sigillum Apposui Rogatus.[134]

Hen[ri]cus Smith Not[ari]us Publ[ic]us
1698

I Thomas Lawrence Notary & tabellion Publick by Royall Authority Admitted And Sworn dwelling in London do hereby Certifye And Attest unto All whome it may Concern that I have Seen And Perused Certayn Letters Patents of Denization Granted by our Sovereign Lord King William the third under the broad Seal of England dated the 11th: day of March in the 12th: year of his majties: Reign wherein Among others is Incerted the name of John Green Alias Vert who though born Beyond Seas is made his majties: Leige Subject And is to be held Reputed And taken as a Subject born in this Kingdom of England And may as Such purchase buy Sell and dispose of Lands tenaments Heriditaments in this Kingdom or in any other of his majties dominions as freely peaceably & Intirely as Any Subject Born in this Kingdom And that the sd: John Green Alias Vert by Virtue of the sd. Letters Patents is to Enjoy All Libertyes priviledges And Franchises of Subject Born in this Kingdom without Any disturbance Impedimt or molestation as Also permitting the persons in the sd: Patent mentioned to be Marriners or masters of Ships dureing the time they And their familyes Shall Reside & Inhabit within the dominions of the Crown of England And no Longer as by the sd. Patent Relation being thereunto had may more at Large Appear, of all wch Act being Required of me the sd Notary I have Granted these presents to Serve And Avail the sd: John Green Alias Vert In time And place Convenient London the 20th day of March 1699 And in the twelfth year of his majties: Reign.

Seal [135]
In Testimonium Veritatis Signo meo manuali Solito Signavi & Tabellionatus mei Sigillum apposui Rogatus.[136]

Tho Lawrence
1699 Not[ariu]s Pub[li]cus

As Also the fredom of the sd: Ship st: Peter Anthony of London undr: the hand And Seal of office of Sr: John Shaw Barronett Collector of his majties. Customs Inward in the Port of London dated the 22th. day of July one thousand Six hundred And ninety Six in the Eight year of his majties. Reign whereby is Certyfyed that the sd: Daniell Perreau is a free Denizon And Sole owner thereof.

As Also A Mediterreanean pass[137] for the sd. Ship st: Peter Anthony whereof

[133] See note 131 above.
[134] See note 132 above.
[135] See note 131 above.
[136] See note 132 above.
[137] A Mediterranean pass was one that guaranteed protection against Algerine pirates. It was issued by the Admiralty, under treaty arrangements with the Barbary states.

Daniel Perreau is master by the Commissionrs. for Executeing the office of Lord high Admirall of England dated the fourteenth day of June 1700.

As Also the Registr: of the sd: Ship In these Words

In Pursuance of Act made Anno Septimo et Octavo Gulielmi 3d: Regis Intitulled An Act for preventing frauds And Regulateing Abuses in the Plantation trade

Jurat Daniel Perreau of London merchant that the Ship the Peter And Anthony Gally of London whereof John Thomas is at Present mastr: being a Squear Stern Ship of one hundred tuns or thereabouts was taken & Condemned for Prize In the high Court of Admiralty of England the 19th: January 1692 And that Daniel Perreau is at present the Sole owner thereof And that no Foreigner directly or Indirectly hath any Share or Part or Intrest therein Dated at the Custom House London the 12th: day of Janry: 1697.

Seal
J Crisp
pro Collr.[138]

Seal
Ri Mounteney
pro Compt:

Nic: Crisp Collr

Endorst on the back of the Register
Daniel Perreau

Whereas Jno: Thomas was master of the within mentioned Ship at the date of the Registr: thereof but he haveing quitted the Ship Daniel Perreau is become mastr. Endorst 29th: June 1700

Witness Charles Crisp
John Acton

J Adrian D Cust & Collr

Whereupon it is Considerd And the Judgment of the Court is That the Said Ship St: Peter Anthony whereof the Said Daniel Perreau is master be Accquitted And the Said Ship is hereby Acquitted And Discharged from the Said Seizure and Prosecution.

Edw: Hill

Copy
Miles Cary Register

There is no indication that the Court of Vice–Admiralty sat in 1700 after this trial. Edward Hill, the judge, died on November 30, 1700. Miles Cary, the register, was relieved of the office at his own request on December 27, 1700.[139] The trial of the *St. Peter & Anthony* therefore appears to mark the end of the court's proceedings under its original officers.

[138] The certifications for the collector and the comptroller stand in the margin of the manuscript beside the text of the register.

[139] Cary asked to be relieved as register because the office was not consistent with his office of naval officer of the district of York River, that he had held since June 8, 1699: he had decided that it was not suitable for the same person to seize vessels as illegal traders and be a party to trying them. *EJC*, I, 449, II, 126.

A CASE OF 1758
IN THE
VICE-ADMIRALTY COURT OF VIRGINIA

SUPPRESSION of trade with the enemy was a serious concern for the British government throughout its long conflict with France, and especially during the climactic struggle of the Seven Years' War. Part of this forbidden trade was carried on from Ireland or from Great Britain itself, but much or even most of it took place in a brisk traffic between British and French colonies in America.[1]

A vessel carrying illegal cargo of food and other goods for the French West Indies, or one loaded with illicit rum, molasses, and sugar from the French islands for the American mainland, was a rich prize for cruisers of the Royal Navy and for privateers. One such prize was the *Prudent Hannah* of Rhode Island, taken by a British cruiser and condemned by the Court of Vice-Admiralty of Virginia in 1758. Original records of the trial have disappeared, but a transcript of the proceedings, evidently one the owners of the vessel intended to use in an appeal, is preserved in the collections of the Rhode Island Historical Society, and is printed below.[2]

The concluding article presents a collection of documents from the files of the Virginia Court of Vice-Admiralty for the years 1770-1775, with a summary account of the nature and procedure of the court, and a brief comment on its officers during those last few years of its existence.[3]

The reader will find that account as appropriate an introduction to a case in admiralty of 1758, presented here, as to the cases heard in 1770-1775, except that of the officers who served the court in 1758, only Benjamin Waller, the advocate, was still an officer in 1770.

In 1758 the judge of the Court of Vice-Admiralty was Peyton Randolph, also attorney general of the colony, who was commissioned as judge

---

1 On colonial trade with the enemy see George Louis Beer, *British Colonial Policy, 1754-1765* (New York, 1933), pp. 72-131.

2 I am obliged to the late Mr. William M. E. Rachal of the Virginia Historical Society for referring me to the transcript.

3 See below, pp. 79-115.

in November 1744.[4] The advocate, Benjamin Waller, had been appointed by Lieutenant Governor William Gooch in September 1742. The register was John Robinson, whom I cannot further identify, and whose term of service is not known. The marshal was John Pearson Webb, probably a young man of Williamsburg, and a shopkeeper there around 1752-1757.[5] In August 1758 these officers were concerned with the suits brought by Captain Julian Legge, appearing before the court to prosecute two vessels for trading with the enemy.

Captain Legge, commanding H.M.S. *Chesterfield,* had come to Virginia early in June 1758 as an escort for the fleet, and on June 18 he wrote from York River to inform the Admiralty of his plan to sail the next day upon a cruise, on this occasion a patrol in search of enemy shipping and vessels engaged in illegal trade or in any other way contravening the law. On August 24 he wrote again to report that he had returned to York River on August 18, bringing in with him a French brigantine from Port au Prince bound for New York under a flag of truce, with six prisoners and a load of rum, sugar, and molasses, and an English brigantine from Rhode Island bound for Port au Prince under a flag of truce, and "deeply laden with all sorts of Provisions, and other necessaries." Legge added that both vessels had been libelled in the Court of Vice-Admiralty in Virginia, and he had no doubt they would be condemned.[6]

On August 26 Paul Tew, captain of the captured English brigantine, the *Prudent Hannah,* wrote to break the news of his misfortune to Obadiah Brown & Co., the owners. He had been taken by the *Chesterfield,* he wrote, four days after he sailed from Narragansett Bay, and brought into York River, although he first begged Captain Legge to let him go free, and then, when he saw that plea was useless, tried to persuade Legge to send him into some port to the northward (where I imagine he hoped to find some business connection of his owners to call on for help). Tew went on to complain that Legge had promised him liberty to go ashore when they arrived and arrange for his defense, but nevertheless had confined him aboard the

---

[4] His commission as judge of vice-admiralty, dated November 21, 1744, is in the Public Record Office, London (hereafter cited as P.R.O.), H.C.A. 50/10, f. 211; his commission from George III, dated July 25, 1761, is in P.R.O., H.C.A. 50/11, f. 152.

[5] A John Pearson Webb, born in South Farnham Parish, Essex County, on February 1, 1737, was the son of Isaac Webb and his wife Frances, née Barber. I suppose it was this John Pearson Webb and his mother who advertised millinery and other goods for sale in the *Virginia Gazette* for July 10, 1752, and on April 22, 1757, published notice in the paper that Frances had given up the millinery business and moved to the country, while John Pearson remained in Williamsburg to deal with debtors and creditors. It is likely that this young man was the marshal.

[6] See Legge's letters of June 18 and August 24, 1758, to John Clevland, P.R.O., Adm.1/2047 (no page or folio numbers).

Chesterfield for thirty-six hours after their arrival in Virginia. During that time Legge went up to Williamsburg and engaged all the noted attorneys except one. Moreover, Legge had published in the newspaper the report that Tew carried a cargo of provisions, and so misrepresented him to the merchants and gentlemen of Williamsburg that they looked on him as an enemy and a traitor and refused to have anything to do with him. While Tew was still detained aboard the *Chesterfield,* the marshal of the Vice-Admiralty Court seized the *Prudent Hannah* and summoned her captain to appear in court six days later. Before the trial began Tew was able to persuade George Wythe to undertake the defense of the *Prudent Hannah* and her cargo.[7]

The trial opened on August 25 with the submission of libel, answer, and documentary evidence, the advocate's reply, and arguments of counsel continuing through two days, at the end of which the judge ordered the vessel and cargo to be forfeited, appraised, and sold. On the third day of the trial, the judge pronounced the final decree, by which the net proceeds of sales were divided among the king, the libellant, and Lieutenant Governor Francis Fauquier. This is the full account of the proceedings:[8]

Virginia sct. At a Court of Vice Admiralty held at the Capitol in the City of [seal][9] *Williamsburgh on Friday the Twenty fifth day of August In the thirty second Year of the Reign of our Sovereign Lord George the second by the Grace of God of Great Britain France and Ireland King Defender of the Faith &c. And in the Year of our Lord One Thousand seven hundred and fifty eight.*

Before,

Peyton Randolph Esqr. Commissary and Judge of the said Court.

The Court being opened The Marshal made return of a Citation lately issued against the Brigantine Prudent Hannah of Rhode Island together with her Guns Rigging Tackle Apparel Furniture and Lading and also against Paul Tew late Master

[7] On Obadiah Brown & Co., and particularly their ventures in prohibited trade, see James Blaine Hedges, *The Browns of Providence Plantations* (Providence, Rhode Island, 1968), I, 47-69. I am indebted to Dorothy Twohig, associate editor of the *Papers of George Washington,* for directing me to the Brown Papers (hereafter cited as Brown), and I am grateful to the John Carter Brown Library, Brown University, for copies of letters from the Brown Papers and for permission to quote from them. Tew's account of his capture and subsequent troubles is drawn from his letter of August 26, 1758, to Obadiah Brown & Co., from Williamsburg (Brown, L 58-84 Priv.).

[8] The text of the proceedings is that of a copy in the Obadiah Brown Papers, Rhode Island Historical Society. I want to express my gratitude to the Society for a copy of the proceedings and for permission to publish them. In my transcription I have aimed to follow the manuscript faithfully, except that I have brought superscript letters down to the line, expanded (with square brackets) a few words, rendered by *per* the conventional abbreviation of the word, straightened some columns in the appraisal and account of sales, and indented every paragraph.

[9] The wafer seal of the Vice-Admiralty of Virginia is affixed here.

of the said Brigantine which together with the return thereon endorsed being read, Personally Appeared Benjamin Waller Esqr. Advocate of this Court and exhibited the following Libel, to wit, Before you Payton Randolph Esqr. his Majesty's Commissary and Judge of the Court of Vice Admiralty of the Colony and Dominion of Virginia Cometh Julian Legge Esqr. Commander of His Majesty's Ship of War Chesterfield and gives the Court to understand and be informed that the said Julian Legge the Twelfth day of August in the Year of our Lord One Thousand seven hundred & Fifty eight on the High Seas in the Latitude of 36° 30′ North about fifty Leagues from Cape Hatteras and within the Jurisdiction of this Court Seised the Brigantine Prudent Hannah of Rhode Island whereof Paul Tew was late Master with all her Guns Tackle Apparel Furniture and lading For that the said Paul Tew did between the Twentieth Day of July in the Year aforesaid and the Day of the Seisure aforesaid at Rhode Island aforesaid,[10] to wit, at the Port of York River in this Colony and within the Jurisdiction of this Court load or Cause to be Laden on board the said Brigantine whereof he was then Master several Barrels of Flour Bread Biscuit Beef Pork and other sort of Victual Particularly expressed and mentioned in the Schedule No. 1 hereto annexed during the Continuance of the Present War with France & did export Transport carry and Convey the same out of and from Rhode Island aforesaid being one of the British Colonies or Plantations in America in the Brigantine aforesaid in Order to Carry the same to Port au Prince in the Island of Hispaniola Contrary to the form of the Statute in that case made and Provided by which the said Brigantine and all her Guns Tackle Apparel and Furniture and the Victuals aforesaid are forfeited one Moiety thereof to His Majesty and the other Moiety to the said Julian Legge who as well for our Lord the King as himself Prosecutes And for that the goods wares and Merchandizes Particularly expressed & mentioned in the Schedule No. 2 hereto also annexed with divers other goods wares and Merchandizes now on board the said Brigantine were Shipped and put on board the said Brigantine within the time herein before mentioned to be carried forth to the open Sea from Rhode Island aforesaid to be landed at some other of the British Plantations in America without a Sufferance or Warrant first had and obtained from the Person or Persons appointed for Managing the Customs and Officers of his Majesty's Customs whereby the said Goods Wares and Merchandizes are forfeited one third thereof to our said Lord the King one other third thereof to the Honorable Francis Fauquier Esqr. His Majesty's Lieutenant Governor and Commander in Chief of this Dominion & the other third to the said Julian Legge who as well for our said Lord the King and the said Lieutenant Governor as himself Prosecutes Wherefore the said Julian Legge prays the Advice of the Court in the Premises and so forth.

The Schedule No. 1 to which the Libel refers. 46 Barrels of Flour 37 Barrels of Beef and Pork. 213 Barrels and 9 Hogsheads of Fish 4 firkins of Butter 2 Barrels of

---

[10] The eighteen words from this point on through "Court" make no sense. Apparently they were included by mistake, but they may be the remnant of a longer passage that would have made sense.

Beans 1500 Weight[11] Sea Bread 3 Barrels of Hogs Heads and Heels, 1000 Bunches of Onions.

The Schedule No. 2 to which the Libel refers. 6 Barrels of Flour 4 Barrels of Beef 2 Pipes Vidona Wine 3 Barrels of Hogs Heads & Heels 7 Boxes Wax Candles 7 Box's Sperma Cetae Candles 1 Mahogony Desk a Parcel of Mens Shoes 10 Barrels of flour 8 Barrels of Beef 2 Box's Sperma Cete Candles 6 Barrels of Pickled Fish 1 Maple Desk 1½ Dozen Chairs & other Goods 34,000 Lumber[12] 14 Desks 1000 Bunches of Onions 6 Box's Soap 19 Casks Wine 8 Barrels of Oyle 5 Casks Beer 24 Box's Candles 207 Barrels & 9 Hogsheads of Fish. Which together with the Libel aforesaid being read The said Paul Tew appeared by George Wythe one of the Proctors of this Court and prayed time 'til Tomorrow to Answer the said Libel.

Ordered That the Court be Adjourned 'til Tomorrow Morning ten of the Clock.

Saturday August the 26th. 1758

Present,

Peyton Randolph Esqr. Commissary and Judge of this Court.

The Court being Opened The said Paul Tew Appeared and filed the following Answer, to wit, The Answer of Paul Tew late Master of the Brigantine Prudent Hannah of Rhode Island to the Libel exhibited against the said Brigantine and her lading by Julian Legge Esqr. Commander of his Majesty's Ship of War Chesterfield. This respondent for answer to the said Libel saith he Admits it to be true that the Libellant on the fifteenth day of August in the Year of our Lord one thousand seven hundred and fifty eight on the high Seas in the Latitude of [ ] & Longitude of [ ][13] within the Jurisdiction of this Court did Seise the Brigantine Prudent Hannah of Rhode Island whereof this Respondent was then Master with all her Tackle apparel Furniture and Lading which Lading as well as this respondent can remember, consisted of the following articles, to wit, thirty four Thousand boards and Shingles, fourteen Desks made at Rhode Island one Thousand bunches of Onions six Box's of Soap nineteen Casks (two of which were Pipes) of French Wine which had been taken and in the Court of Vice Admiralty of Rhode Island condemned as Prize eight barrels of Oyl five Casks of bottled beer twenty four Boxes of Candles two hundred and seven barrels and nine hogsheads of fish (all which were entered and cleared at his Majesty's Custom House in Rhode Island according to Law for the Island of Jamaica being one of His Majestys Colonies or Plantations in America as by a Certificate from the Officers of the Customs there which this Respondent delivered to the Libellant, and to which when produced he this Respondent craves leave to refer as part of his Answer will Appear) forty five or six Barrels of flour, thirty seven barrels of beef and Pork four firkins of butter two barrels of beans fifteen hundred pounds weight of Sea Bread, three Barrels of Hogs heads and Heels seven

---

[11] Or 15 hundredweight. The hundredweight, here a measure of weight of 100 lbs., was usually abbreviated as *cwt*, but in this manuscript as *ct*.

[12] Tew's answer described this lumber as 34,000 boards and shingles; it appears in the appraisal and account of sales as 23,000 shingles and 4909 feet of plank or boards.

[13] Blank spaces in the manuscript. In his letter of August 26 (cf. note 7 above) Tew gave his position as lat. 36° 50′ long. "71 & odd."

box's of Wax Candles & nine Boxes of Sperma Cete Candles one Mahogony Desk a parcel of Mens Shoes six Barrels of Pickled fish one maple Desk and six chairs with flagged Seats besides which for any thing this respondent knows to the Contrary, there might be some trifling things belonging to some of the foremast Seamen of the said Brigantine which were not entered and Cleared But this Respondent humbly insists that the said Brigantine and her tackle Apparel Furniture and Lading are not forfeited for he further Answering says that in Pursuance of an Act of the General Assembly of Rhode Island by a certain Writing bearing Date the twenty fifth Day of July in the Year aforesaid reciting among other things that this respondent master of the Brigantine aforesaid was going with a Flag of truce from Rhode Island unto Port au Prince in the Island of Hispaniola and carried with him fifteen French Prisoners and that Daniel Jenckes & Elisha Brown who subscribed their Names to the said Writing were appointed by the General Assembly of Rhode Island to examine every flag of truce that should be fitted out at that Port and also to see that no goods be put on board contrary to Law the said Daniel Jenckes and Elisha Brown certified that the Brigantine aforesaid had not on board any Goods contrary to Law that there were twenty five barrels of beef and Pork and thirty barrels of flour fifteen hundred pounds weight of Sea Bread four firkins of Butter and two barrels of beans which said Quantity of Provision in their Opinion was no more than a sufficiency for a Subsistence of the said Paul Tew his People and the Prisoners in their Voiage to Port au Prince for him and his People whilst they should tarry there and to support them in their Voiage homeward, with fifteen British Subjects whom he was to bring from thence if there were so many Prisoners at Port au Prince. In Consequence of which last mentioned certificate the Honorable Stephen Hopkins Esqr. Governor Captain General and Commander in Chief of and over the English Colony of Rhode Island and Providence Plantations in New England in America by a Certain Instrument of Writing under the Seal of that Colony bearing Date the twenty sixth day of July in the Year aforesaid and Signed by the said Governor reciting it to be the custom & usage of Nations at War to exchange such Prisoners as the Parties take from each other and to that end the Subjects and vessels of one Prince were by way of truce admitted into the Territories Ports and Harbours of the Prince with whom he was at enmity and that there were Several of the Subjects of his Most Christian Majesty at that time Prisoners of War in that Colony who were desirous of being exchanged for British Subjects Prisoners of War among the French therefore that such an exchange might be made as it tended to the reciprocal advantage of those who by the fortune of War had been deprived of their Liberty the said Governor in the Name of his British Majesty did Authorize and impower this respondent to take on board the said Brigantine all French Subjects that were Prisoners of War in that Colony and such others as he might find elsewhere with such Stores and Necessaries as the Voiage required and with them proceed directly to Port au Prince in the Island of Hispaniola in the West Indies with a flag of truce and there deliver up the said Prisoners and receive such and so many British Prisoners as should be given in exchange for them or such other Prisoners as had been theretofore released without consideration by that Colony since the Commencement of the Present War As by the said last mentioned Certificate Authenticated by a Testimonial under the Hand and

Notorial Seal of Office of Thomas Ward Esquire Secretary and Public Notary of the said Colony and the said Instrument of Writing signed by Governor Hopkins to which in the Custody of the Libellant this respondent also craves leave to refer as part of his Answer may among other things more fully Appear After which the Respondent received on board the said Brigantine fifteen French Prisoners at Rhode Island (as will Appear by a writing under the Hand and Seal of Office of the said Secretary also in the Libellants Custody and referred to) and was proceeding in his Voiage when the said Brigantine was Seised by the Libellant. And this respondent further Answering saith that the beef Pork and flour mentioned in the said first certificate are part of the Commodities of that kind above said not to be entered and Cleared & that the residue of them and of the others not entered and Cleared were the Property of this Respondent and his two Mates who had the Privilege from their Owners of making what Advantage they could by such private Adventures which it is not usual to enter or clear out at the Custom Houses in Rhode Island Wherefore this Respondent prays to be hence dismissed with his Costs.

Sworn to in Court Augst. 26th. 1758. PAUL TEW

JOHN ROBINSON Reg[iste]r

The Papers referred to in the Answer of the Respondent are as follows (Vizt.).

Whereas Paul Tew of Providence in the County of Providence and Colony of Rhode Island Master of the Brigantine called the Prudent Hannah is going with a Flagg of Truce from this Port unto Port au Prince on the Island of Hispaniola and carries with him fifteen french Prisoners besides himself and People consisting of Ten Men inclusive, and whereas we the Subscribers are Appointed by the General Assembly of the Colony aforesaid to examine every Flagg of Truce that shall be fitted out at this Port and also to see that no Goods be put on board contrary to Law We have undertaken that Service and do hereby Certifie that the Brigantine aforesaid hath not on Board any Goods contrary to Law, There is indeed twenty five Barrels of Beef and Pork Thirty Barrels flour Fifteen hundred weight of Sea Bread four Firkins of Butter and two Barrels of Beans which said Quantity of Provisions in our Opinion is no more than a Sufficiency for the Subsistance of the said Paul Tew his People and the said Prisoners in their Voiage to the said Port au Prince, for him and his People whilst they tarry there and to Support them in their Voiage Homeward with fifteen British Subjects whom he is to bring from thence if there be so many of them Prisoners at said Port au Prince. Given under our Hands July the 25th. 1758.

DANIEL JENCKES
ELISHA BROWN

To all unto whom these Presents shall come Thomas Ward of Newport in the County of Newport in the English Colony of Rhode Island and Providence Plantations in New England in America Esquire Secretary and Publick Notary of the said Colony duly elected and engaged according to Law sends Greeting Know ye that Daniel Jenckes and Elisha Brown both of Providence in the County of Providence and Colony aforesaid Esquires who have made and Signed the Certificate written and contained in and upon the other side of this half Sheet of Paper were to my own certain Knowledge which is founded on the Records of this Colony (in my Office as Secretary being) Chosen unto and do actually sustain the Office within mentioned. Wherefore unto their said Certificate full Faith and absolute Credit is and ought to be given by all Persons universally of every Order Rank and Degree whatsoever.

(L.S.) In Witness whereof I do hereunto set my Hand and Affix the Notarial Seal in my Office the twenty sixth Day of July in the Year of our Lord One Thousand seven hundred and fifty eight and thirty second of the Reign of his most Sacred Majesty George the Second by the Grace of God King of Great Britain and so forth.

THO: WARD

(L.S.) By the Honble Stephen Hopkins Esqr. Governor Captain General and Commander in Chief of and over the English Colony of Rhode Island and Providence Plantations in New England in America.

To all unto whom these Presents shall come Greeting.

Forasmuch as it is the Custom and Usage of Nations at War to exchange such Prisoners as the Parties take from each other And to that end the Subjects and Vessels of one Prince are by way of Truce Admitted into the Territories Ports and Harbours of the Prince with whom he is at Enmity, And as there are several of the Subjects of His Most Christian Majesty at this Time Prisoners of War in the Colony aforesaid who are desirous of being exchanged for british Subjects Prisoners of War among the French Now to the End such an Exchange may be made as it tends to the reciprocal Advantage of those who by the fortune of War have been deprived of their Liberty Be it known and Manifest that I the Governor above named have Authorized and in the Name of my Sovereign George the second by the Grace of God of Great Britain and so forth do hereby Authorize & Impower Paul Tew Master of the Brigantine called the Prudent Hannah of the Burthen of Sixty five Tons or thereabouts by Register to take on Board his said Vessel all French Subjects that are Prisoners of War in this Colony and such others as he may find elsewhere with such Stores and Necessaries as the Voiage may require and with them proceed directly to Port au Prince on the Island of Hispaniola in the West Indies with a Flag of Truce and there deliver up the said Prisoners and receive such and so many British Prisoners as shall be given in exchange for them or such other Prisoners as have been heretofore Released without Consideration by this Colony since the Commencement of the Present War And I do hereby strictly Inhibit and forbid the said Paul Tew to receive take or lade or suffer be received taken or laden on Board his Vessel aforesaid any Military Force or Warlike Stores or other Goods Merchandizes or Effects whatsoever contrary to Law not doubting that the Supreme Officer at Port au Prince aforesaid & all others unto whom it doth or shall Appertain will grant him the said Paul Tew and his People all due and Necessary Assistance and Protection And also according to the Established custom supply him with Necessaries sufficient for the bringing himself and his People with such British prisoners unto their own

Country And I do farther desire and request all Commanders of Vessels of Force and others that may meet with the Vessel aforesaid on its Passage either going or returning to or from the said Port au Prince to exempt her and the People on Board from all manner of Force or Constraint according to the Law of Nations.

And that the Truth hereof may be fully Established I sign this Instrument and cause the Seal of the Colony aforesaid to be Affixed the twenty sixth day of July in the Year of our Lord One thousand seven hundred and fifty eight and thirty second of the Reign of my Sovereign aforesaid.

By his Honor's Command STEP: HOPKINS

THO. WARD Secr[etar]y

To all unto whom these Presents shall come Thomas Ward of Newport in the County of Newport in the English Colony of Rhode Island and Providence Plantations in New England in America Esqr. Secretary and Public Notary of the said Colony duly elected and engaged according to Law sends Greeting Know ye that Paul Tew of Providence in the County of Providence & Colony aforesaid Mariner who at Present is Master of a certain Brigantine called the Prudent Hannah of the Burthen of Sixty five Tons or thereabouts by Register having this twenty sixth day of July in the Year of our Lord One Thousand seven hundred and fifty eight and thirty second of the Reign of His Most Sacred Majesty George the second by the Grace of God King of Great Britain and so forth given Bond according to Law in the Secretary's Office hath rec[eiv]ed of the Honble Stephen Hopkins Esqr. Governor of the Colony aforesaid an Instrument in Writing under the Seal of the said Colony by the said Governor Signed and bearing even Date herewith whereby he the said Paul Tew is Authorized to embarque in the Vessel aforesaid and proceed with a flag of truce unto Port au Prince on the Island of Hispaniola carrying with him fifteen of His most Christian Majesty's Subjects who by the fortune of War have been taken Prisoners and brought into this Colony their Names are as followeth, to wit, Louis Blanchet, Edem Patris, Francois Lagarde, Francois Parioleau Jean Pringau Joseph Morise Pierre Savariau Simon Doriae Jean Cloue Pierre Descoufaire Pierre Arrive, Jean Latous, Joseph Desfossez, Jean Hardy J Batiste Roullan For whom the said Paul Tew is to receive in exchange an equal Number of British Subjects if there be so many of them Prisoners at the said Port au Prince Now Know ye that the said Paul Tew hath done and performed all and every the Act and Acts matter and matters Thing and things by Law required in the case of a Flag of truce It is therefore requested and expected of all British Subjects and others who may meet him the said Paul Tew either in his Passage from hence or Voiage homeward to Treat him his People and all others who shall be on board the Brigantine aforesaid according to the Laws of Nations.

(L.S.) Given under my Hand and Seal of Office the Day & Year in these Presents first mentioned.

THO. WARD

Newport, Rhode Island

(L.S.) These are to certify all whom it doth concern That Paul Tew Master or Commander of the Brigantine Prudent Hannah Burthen Sixty five Tons, or Thereabouts mounted with no Guns, navigated with Ten Men Plantation built as per Register Bound for Jamaica having on board Thirty four Thousand of Lumber fourteen Desks made here One Thousand bunches of Onions Six Boxes of Soap and nineteen Casks of Wine Prize Goods here Legally condemned in the Court of Admiralty Eight Barrels of Oyle five Casks of Beans twenty four Boxes of Candles two Hundred and seven Barrels and Nine Hogsheads of Fish. Hath entered and Cleared at His Majesty's Custom House in Rhode Island, according to Law Given under our Hands and Seals of Office this twenty second Day of July in the thirty second Year of the Reign of our Sovereign Lord George the second King of Great Britain and so forth Annoq: Dom: 1758.

J. WANTON Coll[ecto]r

(L.S.) GEO: GARDNER N[aval] Off[ice]r

To which Answer the Advocate replied generally and thereupon the Parties being fully heard by their Counsel The Judge after Mature deliberation Pronounced the following Decree Upon Consideration of the Libel, Answer, the Papers Produced and read and the Arguments of the Counsel on both sides I am of Opinion and do Accordingly Order and Decree That the said Brigantine Prudent Hannah together with her Guns Rigging Tackle Apparel Furniture and Lading be and remain Forfeited one half of the said Vessel and the Victual on board the same to our Sovereign Lord the King and the other half thereof to Julian Legge Esquire the Prosecutor in this Cause And as to the remainder of the Lading one third Part thereof to our said Lord the King one third part thereof to the Honorable Francis Fauquier Esquire Lieutenant Governor and Commander in Chief of this Colony and the other third Part to the said Julian Legge. And I do Order that the said Brigantine together with her Guns Rigging Tackle Apparel Furniture and Lading be Appraised in Current Money by any three of the following Persons, Vizt., Thomas Reynolds David Jameson Edmund Tabb William Stevenson Nicholas Dickson and Robert Ballard Merchants they being first sworn before a Justice of the Peace for York County for that Purpose and after such Appraisment that the Marshall Sell the same to the Highest bidder for ready Money and that he make return of his Proceedings therein to this Court on the Nineteenth Day of September next in Order to a final Decree.

Ordered That the Court be Adjourned 'til the 19th. Day of September next.

Wednesday September the 19th. 1758.

Present,

Peyton Randolph Esqr. Commissary and Judge of this Court

The Court being Opened The Marshal returned the Appraisment and Account of Sales of the Brigantine Prudent Hannah and her Cargo Pursuant to the last Decree in this Cause, which said Accounts being examined and Approved by the Judge, were Ordered to be Lodged in this Court. Then the Judge Pronounced this final Decree,

I Do Decree and Order That the Marshal of this Court after deducting Sixty six Pounds two Shillings his Account of Charges Twenty one Pounds fifteen Shillings and three pence for Duties on the Liquors and twelve pounds ten Shillings The Usual Fee to the Judge and other Officers of the Court, Pay unto our Sovereign Lord the King four hundred and fifty Nine Pounds ten shillings and ten pence, To the Honorable Francis Fauquier Esquire Lieutenant Governor one hundred and twenty seven pounds two shillings and four pence, and to Julian Legge Esquire the Prosecutor four hundred and fifty nine Pounds ten shillings and ten pence for their respective parts of the said Vessel and her Cargo.

From which Decree Paul Tew late Master of the said Brigantine (on behalf of the owners of the said Vessel and Cargo) Prayed an Appeal to the Commissioners Appointed for receiving hearing and Determining Appeals in Causes of Prizes which was granted him upon his giving Bond with sufficient Security on or before the first Day of December next to Prosecute the same with Effect and to pay all such Costs & Damages as shall be awarded ag[ain]st him by the said Commissioners in Case the Decree aforesaid shall be Affirmed.[14]

Appraisment of the Brigantine Prudent Hannah and her Cargo.

The Brigantine with her Furniture			£400.—.—
74 Bundles Hoops		@ 1/	3.14.—
8 Barrels fish Oil		@ £3	24.—.—
14 Maple and Cedar Desks		£2	28.—.—
1 Mahogany Do.			3.10.—
1 Maple Table			—.15.—
1 Mahogany Do.			1. 5.—
18 Chairs		@ 2/	1.16.—
5 Casks Beer Q[uanti]ty 61 dozn. 11 Bottles		@ 10/	30.19. 2
6 Boxes Soap	Wt. 315 lb.	8d	10.10.—
45 Boxes Sperma Ceti Candles	Wt. 1321¾ lb.	@ 1/4	87.12. 4
3 Boxes large Do.	138.1 N[15]	1/	6.18. 3
7 empty Butts		4/	1. 8.—
3 empty Barrels		2/6	—. 7. 6
2 Pipes Wine		@ £20	40.—.—

[14] In his letter of August 22, cited in note 7 above, Tew informed his owners that he had received permission to appeal on condition he produced bond for £100 sterling within fourteen days after the sale of the *Prudent Hannah* and her cargo on September 19, as security that he would prosecute the appeal within twelve months (from the date of the bond, presumably). This permission to appeal indicated in the foregoing paragraph was evidently granted on or after September 30, the date of Littleton Eyre's bond, the last document in the proceedings. I assume the date here mentioned as limiting the appeal was December 1, 1759, and final permission to appeal was, for some reason, granted as late as December 1, 1758; such a delay in granting permission would explain why the proceedings did not come to the agent in Philadelphia for Obadiah Brown & Co., Tench Francis, before January 10, 1759. I do not understand why both Tew and Francis described the amount of the bond as £100 sterling, while the copy of the bond with the proceedings states the amount to be £200 sterling. The letters of October 27, 1758, and January 10, 1759, from Tench Francis to Obadiah Brown & Co. are in Brown, L 58-87 TF.

[15] The last digit of the weight, ".1," stands for one quarter. The *N* following the weight should probably have been @.

7 Boxes Wax Candles	Weight 143 lb. 1 Qr. @ 1/		7. 3. 3
1 Barrel Turpentine			—.15.—
2 Barrels Nails	Wt. 325 lb.	@ 30/ per Ct.	4.17. 6
23 M Shingles		8/ per M	9. 4.—
4909 Feet Plank		40/ per M	9.16. 4
17 Hhds Claret		80/	68.—.—
7 Barrels Syder[16]		10/	3.10.—
58 Pair Mens Shoes[17]		5/	14.10.—
1 Barrel Tarr			—.10.—
11 Casks Ship Bread	Wt. 2872 Nt.	@ 10/ per Ct.	14. 7. 2
17 Barrels Beef		@ 20/	17.—.—
13 Barrels Pork		35/	22.15.—
50 Barrels Flour	11108 lb. Nt.	10/ per Ct.	55.10. 9
1 Box Cheese	72 lb. Nt.	-/7½ per lb.	2. 5.—
11 Ferkins Butter	Wt. 732 Nt.	@ 4d per lb.	9. 3.—[18]
9 Hogsheads dryed Fish	Wt. 7942 Nt.	8/4 per lb.[19]	33. 1.10
93 Barrels Mackrael		@ 12/6 Bl.	58. 2. 6
108 Barrels Manheadon		10/ Bl.	54.—.—
1 Iron Pott			—.10.—
2 Boxes Tallow Candles bad	Wt. 47 lb.[20]	4d per lb.	—.15. 8
Onions[21]			4.—.—
			£1030.12. 3

Pursuant to an Order of the Court of Vice Admiralty We the Subscribers being first Sworn have Appraised the Brigantine Prudent Hannah and her Cargo as above.

Septr. 9th. 1758.

EDMD. TABB
NICHOLAS DICKSON
WILLM. STEVENSON

An Account of Sales of the Brigantine Prudent Hannah and her Cargo.

To Capt. Calvert	The Brig: with her Furniture as per Schedule			£465.—.—
	Provisions.			
Mr. Powell	6 Barrels flour	Wt. 1338 Nt.	@ 13/4[22]	8.18. 4
Mr. Dickson	6 Do. / 6 Do.	2676 Nt.	@ 13/4	17.16. 8
Mr. Dickson	5 Do. / 7 Do. / 7 Do.	4237 Nt.	@ 13/	27.10.10

[16] The account of sales gives 9 barrels.
[17] The account of sales gives 47 pairs and 1 odd shoe.
[18] The correct total is £12.4.0.
[19] The price is 8/4 per hundredweight.
[20] The total weight of candles in this appraisal is 1650¼ lbs.
[21] Not found in the account of sales.
[22] The price of flour and bread in this and the six items following is per hundredweight.

Mr. Tabb	6 Barrels flour	Wt. 1338 Nt.	@ 12/9	8.10. 6
Mr. Dickson	6 Do.	1338 Nt.	@ 12/9	8.10. 6
Mr. Powell	1 Do.	181 Nt.	@ 12/9	1. 3.—
Mr. Tabb	10 Casks & 1 Bar: Bread	2872 Nt.	@ 11/	15.16.—
Mr. Norton	8 Cheese	72	@ 7½d	2. 5.—
Capt. Chisam	11 firkins Butter	732	@ 3¼d	9.18. 3
Mr. Dickson	1 Bbl Pease[23]			—. 6.—
Mr. Phripp	5 Bbls Beef		@ 21/6	5. 7. 6
Mr. Dickson	5 Bbls Do.		@ 22/6	5.12. 6
Do.	7 Bbls Do.			8.10.—
Mr. Heslup	8 Bbls Pork			12.17.10
Mr. Dickson	5 Do.		@ 36/	9.—.—
Capt. Thomson	2 Bbls heads & heels[24]		@ 14/	1. 8.—
Mr. Heslup	1 Do.			—.14.—
Capt. Bevin	10 Bbls McCarell[25]			4. 7. 6
Mr. Rae	10 Do.			4. 5.—
Capt. Miller	10 Do.			4. 8. 6
Mr. Gordon	10 Do.			4.12.—
Mr. Rae	10 Do.			4.12. 6
Capt. Bevin	10 Do.			4.15.—
Mr. Rae	10 Do.			4.15.—
Capt. Chisam	10 Do.			4.18.—
Do.	11 Do.			4.19.—
Mr. Moreland	2 Do. broke			—.10.—
Capt. Bevin	10 Bbls Manhadon			2. 3.—
Capt. Thomson	10 Do.			2. 3. 6
Capt. Chisam	10 Do.			2. 4.—
Mr. Rae	10 Do.			2. 5.—
Do.	10 Do.			2. 5.—
Do.	10 Do.			2. 6.—
Capt. Chisam	10 Do.			2. 1.—
Do.	10 Do.			2. 3.—
Mr. Dickson	16 Do.			2.13. 6
Capt. Chisam	12 Do.			2.10.—
Mr. Gordon	1 hhd dry fish	860 Nt.	8/9[26]	3.14. 9
Mr. Heslup	1 Do.	870 Nt.	9/2	3.19. 9
Mr. Knox	1 Do.	947	9/3	4. 7. 6
Mr. Tabb	1 Do.	909	9/7	4. 6.10
Mr. Gordon	1 Do.	800	10/4	4. 2. 8

[23] Not in the appraisal.
[24] Not in the appraisal.
[25] Mackerel.
[26] The price here and in the eight items following is per hundredweight.

Mr. McCaul	1 Do.	883	11/7	5. 1. 2
Mr. Heslup	1 Do.	837	10/4	4. 6. 6
Do.	1 Do.	929	10/2	4.14. 2
Do.	1 Do.	907	11/	4.19. 8
		To be divided in two parts		£713.14. 5[27]
Mr. Scrivener	5 Boxes Sperma Caeti Candles	Wt. 129.0	2/1	13.18. 9[28]
Mr. Dickson	5 Do.	144.2	2/2½	15.19. 1
Mr. McCaul	5 Do.	136.1	2/2½	15.—.11
Mr. Norton	5 Do.	135.3	2/2½	14.19. 9¾
Mr. Mills	4 Do. P.T.[29]	119.3	2/2½	12.14. 5½
P. Grymes Esq:	2 Do. B W[30]	65.3	2/3½	7.10. 7½
Mr. Prentis	3 Do. P T[31]	103.3	2/2	10.16. 2½
Mr. McCaul	1 Do.	48.3	1/8	4. 1. 3
Mr. Phripp	1 Do.	42.1	1/8	3.10. 5
Capt. Legge	1 Do.	47.1	2/1	4.18. 5½
Mr. McCaul	5 Do.	135.3	2/1½	14. 8. 5½
Mr. Scrivener	2 Do. S I[32]	70.3	2/3	7.19. 2
Mr. Penman	1 Do. broke	27.2	2/	2.15.—
Mr. Taylor	4 Do.	99.1	2/2	10.15. 0½
Mr. Balfour	4 Do.	113.3	2/1½	12. 1. 7½
Mr. Trebell	3 Do.	56.1	1/11½	5.10. 2
Mr. Dickson	4 Do.	87.0	1/10	7.19. 6
Capt. Chisam	2 Boxes Ship Candles[33]	47	3d	—.11. 9
Mr. Prentis	2 Boxes Soap	124	12d½	6. 9. 2
Mr. Norton	2 Do.	118.0	1/	5.18.—
Do.	2 Do. broke	73.0	11d½	3.10.—
Do.	2 Bbls Oil			7.14.—
Mr. Dickson	2 Do.			7.17.—
Mr. McCaul	2 Do.			8.—.—
Mr. Prentis	2 Bbls Oil			8. 1.—
Cash	1 Bbl Tar			—.10.—
	1 Do. Turpentine			—.12.—
Capt. Thomson	2 firkins Nails	325	@ 33/ Ct.	5. 7. 3

27 The court decreed that net proceeds of the sale of vessel, tackle, and lading be divided in halves, one for the king and the other for the prosecutor.

28 The correct total is £13.8.9. The final digit in the weight here and in the sixteen items following represents quarters of a pound.

29 Probably Paul Tew's initials as a mark to identify property intended for sale in one of the private ventures he mentioned in his answer as a privilege the owners allowed to him and his two mates.

30 Probably the initials of one of Tew's mates, as a mark to identify his property (cf. note 29 above).

31 Probably Tew's initials (cf. note 29 above).

32 Probably the initials of the other of Tew's mates (cf. notes 29 and 30 above).

33 The total weight of candles in the account of sales is 1610¼ lbs. (cf. note 20 above).

Mr. Powell	1 Iron Pott			—.10. 1
Mr. Knox	6 Pr. Mens Shoes			1. 8.—
Mr. Dickson	6 Pr. Do.			1.11.—
Mr. Gibbons	6 Pr. Do.			1.12. 6
Mr. Tabb	6 Pr. Do.			1. 9.—
Mr. Powell	6 Pr. Do.			1. 6. 6
Mr. Wade	6 Pr. Do.			1.13.—
Mr. Dickson	6 Pr. Do.			1. 7. 6
Mr. Tucker	3 Pr. 1 odd Do.			—.13.—
Mr. Powell	2 Pr. Do.			—.10.—
Mr. Trebell	18 Chairs			1.16.—
Cash	1 Mahogany Table			1.10.—
Mr. Burt	1 Maple Do.			—.16.—
Mr. McCaul	1 Mahogany Desk			5.16.—
Capt. Dickenson	1 Caedar Do.			2. 8.—
Mr. Knox	1 Maple Do.			3. 1.—
Mr. Prentis	1 Do.			2. 1. 6
Mr. Mitchell	1 Do.			2. 4.—
Mr. Rae	1 Do.			2. 5.—
Mr. Sewell	1 Do.			2. 6.—
Mr. Wormeley	1 Do.			2.—. 6
Mr. A Lightfoot	1 Do.			2.15.—
Mr. Trebell	1 Do.			2.13.—
Mr. Penman	1 Do.			2. 8.—
Mr. Powell	1 Do.			2.15.—
Cash	1 Do.			2. 6.—
Mr. Trebell	1 Do.			2. 8.—
Mr. Jameson	1 Do.			2. 5.—
Cash	74 Bundles hoops			3. 8.—
Mr. Wormeley	23 M Shingles		@ 12/6	14. 7. 6
Capt. Mitchell	4909 feet Boards		@ 30/6	7. 9. 8
Mr. Mitchell	14 dozn. 10 Bottles Beer[34]		@ 15/6	11. 9.11
I. P. W.[35]	4 Do.			—. 5.—
Capt. Legge	1 Cask 11 doz. 7 Bottles		14/6	8. 7.11½
P. Grymes Esqr.	1 Cask 8 doz: & 2		14/6	5.17. 5[36]
Revd. Mr. Row	1 Do. 17 doz: 5		15/	13. 1. 3
Mr. Tarpley	1 Do. 9 doz: 7		14/	6.14. 2
Mr. Dickson	9 Bbls Cyder			1. 9.—
Capt. Chisam	1 Hhd. Claret	No. 1 63 Galls.		2.13.—
Do.	1 Do.	2 60½ Do.		2. 8.—
Jno. Randolph Esq.	1 Do.	3 63 Do.		3.12.—
Jas. Burwell	1 Do.	4 63 Do.		3.13.—

[34] The price of beer, when stated, is per dozen.
[35] Perhaps for John Pearson Webb, the marshal.
[36] The correct amount is £5.18.5.

Mr. McCaul	1 Do.	5 60 Do.	4. 8. 7½
Do.	1 Do.	6 59 Do.	4. 3. 3½
Capt. Chisam	1 Do.	7 57 Do.	2. 3. 6
Do.	1 Do.	8 63 Do.	1.17. 6
Mr. Phripp	1 Do.	9 51 Do.	1.19.—
Do.	1 Do.	10 56 Do.	2.15. 6
Capt. Bair	1 Do.	11 59 Do.	3.15.—
Mr. Balfour	1 Do.	12 52 Do.	1.14. 8
Capt. Chisam	1 Do.	13 59 Do.	1. 8.—
Mr. Rae	1 Do.	14 59 Do.	4.10.—
Mr. Taylor	1 Do.	15 63	5.15.—
Capt. Bevin	1 Do.	16 57	2.11.—
Capt. Thomson	1 Do.	17 48	4. 8.—
Mr. Dickson	1 Pipe Vidona	1 106	13. 8. 3
Dr. Riddell	1 Do.	2 106	15.18.—
Tarpley & Knox	7 Empty Butts		1. 8.—
Do.	3 Barrels		—. 7. 6
			£1146.11. 8¾[37]

JOHN PEARSON WEBB Marshall

Know all Men by these Presents that we Julian Legge Esqr. Commander of his Majesties Ship of War Chesterfield and the Honorable Francis Fauquier Esqr. Lieut. Governor and Commander in Chief of the Colony and Dominion of Virginia are held and firmly bound unto Peyton Randolph Esqr. Commissary and Judge of the Court of Vice Admiralty of the Colony and Dominion aforesaid in the full and Just Sum of One Thousand Pounds Sterling to be paid to the said Peyton Randolph his Certain Attorney Ex[ecut]ors Administrators or Assigns To the which Paiment well and truly to be made we bind our selves and each of us our and each of our Heirs Executors & Administrators jointly and severally firmly by these Presents Sealed with our Seals and Dated this twenty third Day of September One Thousand seven hundred and Fifty eight.

The Condition of the above Obligation is such that Whereas upon a Libel exhibited in the Court of Vice Admiralty aforesaid by the said Julian Legge against the Brigantine Prudent Hannah and her Lading. It was Decreed and Ordered that the said Brigantine together with her Guns Rigging Tackle Apparel Furniture and Lading be and remain Forfeited on[e] [38] half of the said Vessel and the Victual on Board the same to our Sovereign Lord the King and the other half thereof to the said Julian Legge And as to the remainder of the Lading one third Part thereof to our said Lord the King one third part thereof to the Honorable Francis Fauquier Esqr. Lieutenant Governor and Commander in Chief of the Colony and Dominion aforesaid and the other third part to the said Julian Legge From which Decree Paul Tew late Master of

[37] The correct total is £1146.4.9¾.

[38] The manuscript has *on*.

the said Brigantine (on behalf of the Owners of the said Vessel & Cargo) hath Appealed to the Commissioners Appointed for receiving hearing and determining Appeals in Causes of Prizes Now if the said Julian Legge shall well and truly pay or Cause to be paid all Monies by him Received as his Proportionable part of the Brigantine Prudent Hannah Arrising from the Sales of the said Vessel and Cargo, to the said Peyton Randolph his Ex[ecut]ors Administrators or Assigns, in Case the Decree aforesaid shall be reversed by the aforesaid Commissioners upon hearing the said Appeal Then the aforesaid Obligation to be void else to remain in full Force.

Sealed & Delivered
In Presence of . . .
JOHN ROBINSON
DAVID BOWMAN

JULIAN LEGGE (L.S.)
FRAN: FAUQUIER (L.S.)

Know all Men by these Presents That I Littleton Eyre of the County of Northampton Gent. am held and firmly bound unto Julian Legge Esqr. Commander of His Majesty's Ship of War Chesterfield in the full and just Sum of two hundred Pounds Sterling to the which Paiment well and truly to be made to the said Julian Legge his certain Attorney Ex[ecut]ors Adm[inistrat]ors or Assigns I bind myself my Heirs Executors and Administrators jointly and severally firmly by these Presents Sealed with my Seal and Dated this thirtieth Day of September One Thousand seven hundred and fifty eight.

The Condition of the above Obligation is such That Whereas Paul Tew late Commander of the Brigantine Prudent Hannah of Rhode Island hath (on behalf of the owners of the said Vessel and her Cargo) Appealed from a Decree of the Court of Vice Admiralty in the Colony of Virginia bearing Date the twenty Sixth Day of August one Thousand seven hundred and fifty eight in a Cause prosecuted ag[ain]st him by the said Julian Legge who as well for our Lord the King and the Honorable Francis Fauquier Esquire His Majesty's Lieutenant Governor and Commander in Chief of the said Colony of Virginia as for himself prosecuted If Therefore the said Paul Tew or any other Person or Persons concerned, shall within the Space of twelve Months next ensuing the Date hereof Prosecute with Effect his said Appeal and shall satisfie and pay to the said Julian Legge who as well &c as afores[ai]d his Executors Administrators or Assigns all such Costs and Damages as shall be Decreed by the Commissioners Appointed for receiving hearing and Determining Appeals in Causes of Prizes in Case the Decree of the said Court of Vice Admiralty of Virginia shall be Affirmed, Then this Obligation to be Void else to remain in full force.

Sealed & Delivered
In Presence of . . .
JOHN ROBINSON

LITTLETON EYRE. (L.S.)

A true Copy.
JOHN ROBINSON,
Reg[iste]r C[ourt of] V[ice] Adm[iral]ty

Tew's letter of August 26 had this to say of George Wythe's defense of the *Prudent Hannah* and her cargo, and the court's decree:

> He made a Tollerable good defence by Arguing the Sacredness of Flaggs of Truce amoung all Civiliz'd Nations, And What provisions &c more than Express'd in the Certificate Insisted was Legall by the Collectors Clearance, but all invain Had Cicero himself been present and Argued the Case wou'd have avail'd Nothing She was this day Condemn'd Vessell & Cargo according to popular Clamour, But as they say agreeable to an Act of parliment made in the year 1756 to prevent the Exportation of provisions from the plantations.[39]

Tew went on to explain that what had added to the "popular Clamour" and hastened the condemnation of the *Prudent Hannah* was Legge's capture of a French vessel from Port au Prince, bound to New York under a flag of truce, with a quantity of molasses, rum, and sugar on board, brought in at the same time as Tew. This vessel had on board some letters for France, "Seting forth the Misarable Condition of the Inhabitants there for Want of Provisions and that they Shou'd Suffer more were they not Releived by Flaggs of Truce." Tew added that the French vessel had been tried on August 26 and it was expected she would be condemned, although the court's decree had not yet been announced.[40]

Any "popular Clamour" against Tew might well have been fed by revelations about prohibited trade under flags of truce, arising from the capture of ships engaged in the trade. In September Governor Fauquier informed the Board of Trade[41] that Captain Legge's captures made it clear a regular trade was carried on between Rhode Island and the French West Indies by ships carrying a few prisoners and supplies of provisions for the French; Rhode Island men had sent four ships from Providence to Boston to pick up sixty French prisoners, who were distributed, fifteen to a ship, as a screen for the four cargoes of provisions intended for Port au Prince. Fauquier quoted passages from letters found on Legge's French prize, and mentioned a third prize, a regular cartel ship between Jamaica and Port au

---

[39] The act was 30 George II c. 9, to prohibit the exportation of various provisions from the American colonies, unless to Great Britain, Ireland, or other American colonies (see Owen Ruffhead, *The Statutes at Large*... [London, 1763-1800], VIII, 19-22).

[40] The letters were probably the two, dated June 13, 1758, from Pavayeau Rousseau & Co., at Port au Prince, one to Messrs. Portier *frères* and the other to M. Charles Chancerel, both at Nantes. Captain Legge enclosed copies of those letters in his of November 22, 1758, to John Clevland (P.R.O., Adm.1/2047 [no folio or page numbers]). A report dated Williamsburg, September 1, printed in the *Pennsylvania Gazette* for September 21, 1758, gave notice that on the preceding Monday (August 28) the Court of Vice-Admiralty had condemned the brig *L'Union,* Captain De St. Arromand.

[41] Fauquier to the Board of Trade, September 23, 1758, P.R.O., C.O.5/1329, ff. 82-85.

Prince, furnished with passports from both the English and the French governor. This ship, "loaded up to the Hatches," was taken by a privateer and brought to Virginia.

Legge's report to the Admiralty, two months later,[42] stated he had learned from the vessel he took (presumably the *Prudent Hannah*) of three or four more vessels of her burthen then loading in Rhode Island with every sort of supplies for the French at Hispaniola, all of them having a manifest and clearance from the collector and naval officer in Rhode Island as if cleared out for Jamaica. The clearance would serve to protect them from English cruisers, while the flag of truce would keep them safe from French cruisers. Legge too mentioned a cartel vessel taken by a privateer (probably the one Fauquier had referred to), brought in, and condemned.

When he wrote to Obadiah Brown & Co. on August 26, Tew informed them he had received permission to appeal, but had no hope of procuring bondsmen in Williamsburg; in the following week he proposed to go to Norfolk, where he had heard there were gentlemen who traded with the northern colonies. He asked for instructions, and for a letter of credit.

The owners replied on September 16, expressing their determination to prosecute the appeal, and transmitted a letter of credit. They gave instructions that as soon as Tew had procured bondsmen, he should obtain a "Copy of the Case and all the Proceedings and return Home as soon as possible." A second letter of the same date informed Tew that the owners would be glad to reach a compromise to keep down their losses, but they were determined to prosecute the appeal if no compromise could be arranged.[43]

What Tew did after he reported his intention of going to Norfolk is matter for conjecture, but it seems that he had nothing to do with the business of arranging bond for prosecution of an appeal, and procuring a transcript of proceedings against the *Prudent Hannah*, all of which was apparently handled by Tench Francis, a Philadelphia merchant and a correspondent of Obadiah Brown & Co. On October 27 Francis wrote to let them know that Colonel Littleton Eyre had given security of £100 sterling for the prosecution of their appeal, while he himself had given a counter-security for the same amount to Mr. Gibson (perhaps John Gibson, also a Philadelphia merchant), at whose request Eyre had acted. Francis expected to receive the papers relating to the case by the next post from Virginia; in a

[42] Legge to John Clevland, November 22, 1758, P.R.O., Adm.1/2047 (no page or folio numbers).

[43] The two letters and the letter of credit are in Brown, V Misc.

postscript to his letter of January 10, 1759, Francis notified Obadiah Brown & Co. that he had received the papers from Colonel Eyre, and would forward them by water, in order to save postage.[44]

Nothing has been found in the Admiralty papers at the Public Record Office, or elsewhere, to suggest that Obadiah Brown & Co. made their appeal against the condemnation of the *Prudent Hannah*. It looks, then, as if the company had lost not only the value of the vessel and her cargo (unless they recovered some part of that loss from insurance), but whatever they may have laid out for picking up the French prisoners and sending them off to Hispaniola, the security given for making an appeal, and presumably the expense of passage for Captain Tew and his company from Virginia to Rhode Island, as well as the modest cost of obtaining a copy of the trial proceedings. Even if the company decided not to appeal the condemnation of the *Prudent Hannah,* however, they kept their transcript of proceedings against the vessel, and thus preserved the only record now known of a prosecution for trading with the enemy conducted in the Court of Vice-Admiralty in Virginia.

[44] The letters are in Brown, L 58-87 TF.

THE COURT OF VICE-ADMIRALTY IN VIRGINIA AND SOME CASES OF 1770-1775

For a long time it was commonly supposed that all records of the Court of Vice-Admiralty in Virginia had disappeared,[1] so that nothing could be known of the court's actions beyond what was revealed by rare mentions in correspondence or the executive journals of the Council of Virginia, or brief notices of trials, and advertisements of sales by the court's decree published in the *Virginia Gazette*. None of these sources could be counted on to provide an altogether trustworthy record of what the court had done. Comments in correspondence might easily be biased, or simply inaccurate. What the Council journal or the *Gazette* had to say about the court's activity would no doubt have been a faithful report of information available, but there is no reason to suppose that either the Council or the newspaper would regularly take notice of the court's business. Much of what the journal or the press might have told us about the court could be lost: the court was active from about March 1698 until the collapse of royal government, but the journals of the Council are missing for about half of the period from May 1754 to May 1776 (there are no journals for meetings between May 7, 1754, and June 10, 1756, between September 15, 1763, and September 5, 1767, and after June 17, 1774), and its proceedings in the meetings for which no journal has survived are unknown except for scattered minutes from 1756 and 1764-1767. The first issue of the *Gazette* appeared in 1736, and the file is nearly complete through 1739, but there are only 17 issues known for the period 1740-1765, with none at all left from 1741-1744, 1747-1750, 1758, 1760, and 1763.

In recent years, however, copies of some of the court's records have come to light. Among the Obadiah Brown Papers in the collections of the Rhode Island Historical Society is a copy of proceedings in the trial, held in 1758, of the Rhode Island brigantine *Prudent Hannah,* owned by Obadiah Brown & Co.[2] The Public Record Office in London has three copies of the order of

[1] A suggestion of what happened to some of the records appears in a letter of March 17, 1771, in the Public Record Office in London (hereafter cited as P.R.O.), Adm. 1/3884, in which Benjamin Waller, lately advocate of the court, referred to "the old Records of the Court of Admiralty, which were burnt in the Capitol in January 1746." That was 1747, according to our present calendar.

[2] The late Mr. William M. E. Rachal of the Virginia Historical Society made me aware of these proceedings.

November 15, 1772, allowing an appeal from the court's decree in the case of Maltby vs. *Molly,* one of those appearing later in this paper, and copies of proceedings in eight cases before the court in 1699-1700.

It now appears that the largest and most varied collection of records of the court, all original documents, is a miscellaneous group from the years 1770-1775, part of the Webb-Prentis Papers in the University of Virginia Library, and seemingly preserved by chance among other legal papers accumulated by long-established families of Tidewater Virginia.[3]

The records consist of forty-one items. These include the proceedings of the court in four cases, and a sheet of notes containing a list of costs, a decree, and miscellaneous matter, evidently notes for the proceedings (now missing) in a fifth case. There are also thirty-three documents relating to these cases in the collection, as well as three separate documents, each the only remnant of papers in the case to which it pertains.[4] The proceedings are drafts, with occasional deletions and insertions. Depositions of witnesses and other documents to be inserted in the finished form of the proceedings are omitted from the drafts, with a parenthetical instruction to insert a document at the appropriate point in the proceedings. Proceedings are in the same hand, probably that of a clerk, while the related documents, all in finished form, are in a number of different hands.

There are extended accounts of the colonial courts of vice-admiralty by Charles M. Andrews and Carl Ubbelohde, and a study by Joseph Henry Smith of appeals from the decrees of those courts.[5] Here it should suffice to describe briefly the jurisdiction of the courts of vice-admiralty, the nature of

---

[3] I am obliged to Miss Helen Troy, formerly of the Manuscripts Department, University of Virginia Library, for bringing these papers to my attention; and I am grateful to the University of Virginia Library for permission to publish them.

[4] The records are printed below except for a pair of accounts, duplicates of those already in the proceedings. In the transcriptions I have brought down superscript letters, expanded a few words not usually abbreviated today, and supplied any period omitted at the end of a paragraph. I have adjusted or supplied indentation for clarity or economy of space. Where I could safely do so, I have supplied, in square brackets, what is lost by damage to the paper, or obviously left out by accident. Blank spaces between square brackets represent gaps in the text where the writer deliberately left a blank space, or where there is a hole in the paper. Notes explain the reason for these gaps, where I could not supply the missing text.

[5] Andrews published his "Vice-Admiralty Courts in the Colonies" as the introduction to Dorothy S. Towle, editor, *Records of the Vice-Admiralty Court of Rhode Island, 1716-1752* (Washington, D.C., 1936); it appears, abridged, as "The Vice-Admiralty Courts," a chapter in Andrews, *The Colonial Period of American History* (New Haven and London, 1938; reprinted New Haven, 1964), IV 222-271. Ubbelohde considered the courts as a force working towards the fall of the colonial régime, in *The Vice-Admiralty Courts and the American Revolution* (Chapel Hill, 1960), but he is at the same time more useful than Andrews on the procedure, officers, and terminology of the courts. Smith's examination of appeals from the courts is in his *Appeals to the Privy Council from the American Plantations* (New York, 1950).

the cases represented by surviving records of the Virginia court, the procedure and terminology of the courts, and the officers of the Virginia court.

Colonial courts of vice-admiralty were, as the name suggests, provincial counterparts of the High Court of Admiralty in London. They were concerned with maritime cases, with men who sailed the seas or were engaged in shipping, and with the legal problems in which their livelihood involved them. A few of these present records of the Virginia court relate to ordinary maritime cases, arising from a lender's suit to recover money supplied to fit a vessel, a mariner's suit to get his wages, and a claim for damages caused by collision. Most of the records are concerned with violations of the trade acts, such as neglecting to have the required ship's papers, or, more often, engaging in illicit trade or smuggling.

In admiralty cases, the person seeking relief, the *libellant,* presented his case to the court in the form of a written document stating his complaint, a *libel.* This libel was produced or read in court by the advocate (or advocate general, or judge advocate), the officer who acted as attorney to the court. The judge then issued to the marshal, the officer who executed the court's orders, a *citation,* which might arrest a vessel or her cargo, or cite her master to appear before the court. Next, the judge issued a *proclamation,* or statement of the libellant's complaint, which was read out in court. The *respondent* (or *claimant*), the defendant at whom the libel was aimed, had the right to submit a *claim* and *answer* in reply to the libel. Both parties, it appears, could be represented in court by a *proctor*, or attorney. The court considered the libel, the answer, depositions, and oral testimony of witnesses, and the judge pronounced his *decree*, or judgment in the case. If the decree entailed the forfeiture and condemnation of a vessel or cargo, the marshal had to give public notice of a sale, see that an appraisal of vessel or cargo was made, and present the appraisal and account of sales to the court.[6] The register, responsible for keeping the records of the court, presumably kept notes for the formal proceedings of the court and had custody of the various documents connected with a trial.

In 1770 the judge of the court of vice-admiralty in Virginia was John Randolph, appointed by royal commission in April 1767, who held office as late as April 1775 and, so far as one can see, until the end of the colonial

[6] Ubbelohde offers a longer survey of the course of litigation through the vice-admiralty courts, with the observation that procedure and terminology varied greatly from colony to colony. My survey aims to present only procedure and terminology found in the Virginia records, or otherwise suggested: for instance, there is no mention in those records of a proctor for the court, but in the letter of March 17, 1771, cited in note 1, Benjamin Waller mentioned the difficulty he had experienced in finding a lawyer to assist him in a prosecution.

era.[7] The other officers of the court were presumably appointed by the governor, lieutenant governor, or acting governor in Virginia. Benjamin Waller was appointed advocate by Lieutenant Governor Sir William Gooch in 1742 and served until January 1771, when he resigned. His successor, Richard Starke, appointed by President William Nelson, was dead by August 1, 1772, when James Hubard took the oaths of office as advocate; it appears that Hubard remained advocate so long as the court continued. Thomas Everard was register as early as 1763 and apparently was still register when the court ceased to function. John Tyler, the marshal, was appointed at an undetermined date; he was dead by the latter part of August 1773 and was followed by James Cocke, presumably the last marshal of the colonial court. Under the date of December 23, 1773, the court's proceedings list James Atherton, crier of the court, among those receiving fees. No other mention of a crier has been found; it may be that he was not considered to be an officer of the court.[8]

---

7 For Randolph's commission, dated April 2, 1767, see P.R.O., H.C.A.50/12 ff. 9-11, 74. I find no evidence to support Ubbelohde's statement that Lord Hillsborough gave Randolph an addition of £200 a year to his salary as attorney general on condition of Randolph's giving up his judgeship. Hillsborough wrote to Lord Botetourt, then governor of Virginia, that a salary for the judge of vice-admiralty would have been approved if he had not learned of the objection to one person's holding that office and the office of attorney general, but thereafter he did not refer to the judgeship. He proposed to offer £200 a year to the attorney general, if Botetourt determined that Randolph agreed with the proposal; Botetourt informed Hillsborough that Randolph was suitably grateful for the offer, and thereupon Hillsborough sent a warrant authorizing the £200 additional salary for Randolph, which he described as "being but a just Acknowledgment of that Gentleman's Merit in his commendable Attachment to Government." Relevant letters are in P.R.O., C.O.5/1347 ff. 122-123, 184-185, 199-200.

8 Randolph, Waller, Everard, and Tyler hardly require identification. Richard Starke, a lawyer, in 1766 was appointed clerk of the committees of privileges and elections, of propositions and grievances, and of correspondence, in the House of Burgesses; his commission as advocate of the court of vice-admiralty was dated January 22, 1771. Starke was probably the author of *The Office and Authority of a Justice of Peace . . .*, published in Williamsburg in 1774. James Hubard may plausibly be identified as the man who was at the College of William and Mary 1753-1755, was married to Frances Morton, and advertised in the *Virginia Gazette* for May 11, 1769, that he proposed to practice law in the county courts in and around Williamsburg, and in the admiralty court. It appears that General Cornwallis appointed Hubard as inspector of refugees in Virginia, and that by December 1781 Hubard was in New York, proposing to go to Jamaica. In April 1782 Hubard received £110 as a suffering loyalist for the period August 24, 1781–March 31, 1782; he died in May 1782. In July 1783, Matthew Hubard, aged 16, the orphan son of James Hubard, asked compensation for the loss of his father's estate in Virginia, where he had been "in great Practice at the Bar." On Hubard as a loyalist see P.R.O., P.R.O. 30/11/6 ff. 1-2, P.M.G.14/72 f. 610, and A.O.12/99 ff. 349-350, A.O.13/3 Folder H. Atherton was, perhaps, the man who in 1756 asked consideration for having been wounded at Braddock's defeat on the Monongahela, in 1762 represented that he had been a guard at the magazine in Williamsburg, in 1767 advertised that misfortune compelled him to give up his carpentry business, and in 1772 sought appointment as doorkeeper to the House of Burgesses (*Journals of the House of Burgesses of Virginia,* edited by J. P. Kennedy and H. R. McIlwaine [Richmond, 1905-1915], *1752-1758*, p. 339, *1761-1762*, p. 163, *1770-1772*, p. 155; *Virginia Gazette* [Purdie and Dixon], June 18, 1767).

The earliest of these surviving records of the Virginia court of vice-admiralty is this libel, presented in 1770 in or before November, in an ordinary marine case involving a bottomry, or mortgage, upon a vessel:

Before you John Randolph Esqr his majesties commissary & judge of the court of Vice admiralty in the colony & dominion of Virginia.

Cometh Logan Gilmour & Co. merchants of the Borough of Norfolk by James Hubard their Proctor, & against the sloop Polly & Fanny, whereof James Mudie is or lately was master & owner, with her tackle apparel & furniture, & all other persons concerned or interested therein. Doth alledge, article, & propound as followeth,

Imprimis, they do propound & alledge, that by the marine laws all ships & vessels in the mercantile employ, together with their guns, tackle apparel & furniture are liable to the payment of all sums of money by any person ad[vanced paid] or disbursed to the Captain or owner for repairs outfits & wages due to the mariners, who were hired to navigate the said ships or vessels, in case they do not desert the same.

Item, that by the marine law the Captain or owner of such ships or vessels have a right to hypothecate, pledge and bottomry the ship or vessel of which he's master or owner as a security for all sums of money which hath been advanced paid or disbursed for the use of such ship or vessel, together with interest for the same, at a reasonable rate proportiond to the risque to be run.

Item that the libellants Logan Gilmour & Co upon the high seas within the jurisdiction of this court did on the fifteenth day of January in the year of our lord 1770 advance, disburse and pay to the said James Mudie master & owner of the said sloop Polly & Fanny ninety three pounds current money of Virginia for the fitting the said sloop to proceed upon a voyage upon the high seas from the said Borough of Norfolk to the island of Nevis, for the repayment of which said sum of ninety three pounds with the praemium of ten pounds for the risque, adventure and hazard of the seas during the voyage aforesaid amounting in the whole to one hundred & thirteen pounds within ten days after the said sloops arrival at the island of Nevis aforesaid the said James Mudie master & owner did hypothecate the said sloop to the said Logan Gilmour & Co by an instrument of hypothecation, commonly calld a bottomry, upon the bottom or keel of the said sloop & upon all her tackle apparel & furniture for the voyage aforesaid bearing date the fifteenth day of January 1770, which said instrument they here bring into court.

Item they declare that the said sloop did arrive at the island of Nevis, & has since made a voyage from thence to this colony, & that they did produce unto the said James Mudie the said instrument of Hypothecation, & demanded the said ninety three pounds with the praemium of ten pounds which he the said James Mudie did refuse payment of.

Wherefore the libellants pray that the said sloop Polly & Fanny with her guns tackle apparel & furniture be condemnd & deliverd up to the libellants, unless the said James Mudie do pay unto them the said one hundred & three pounds with legal interest thereon, or that your honour will make such decree & order in the premisses for the libellants, as shall be just, &c.

No other record of this case is known, but it appears that the sloop was not condemned. In the *Virginia Gazette* (Rind) for November 29, 1770, James Mudie advertised for sale part or the whole of the sloop *Polly & Fanny,* a new vessel, well-fitted, a prime sailer; she had made but one voyage to the West Indies, and her burden was about 3,000 bushels.

The next record of the court is this libel, presented in April 1772, and alleging a violation of the trade acts:[9]

Before you John Randolph Esquire his Majesty's Commissary and Judge of the Court of Vice Admiralty in the Colony and Dominion of Virginia.

Cometh Hyde Parker Esquire Commander of his Majesty's Ship of War the Boston, who as well for our Sovereign Lord the King as for Himself in this behalf prosecutes, and gives the Court to understand and be informed, that the said Hyde Parker being duly Authorized to make Seizures on the fourteenth day of April in the Year of our Lord one thousand Seven Hundred and Seventy two at Sea, to wit, in Chesapeake Bay in the lower district of James River and within the Jurisdiction of this Court Seized the Ship Jenifer whereof James Bartholomew was then Master, and Her lading, for that divers Goods Wares and Commodities, that is to say, 50 Cases of Gin & 20 Casks of Gin together with divers other Goods Wares and Commodities (not bona fide & without fraud laden and Shipped in Great Britain, and brought directly thence and from no other place whatsoever, to this Colony,) were imported and brought in the said Ship into the lower district aforesaid, and within the Jurisdiction aforesaid, between the first day of March in the Year aforesaid and the day of the Seizure aforesaid. Also for that divers Goods, Wares, and Commodities were laded in the said Ship at Rotterdam in Holland and from thence brought in the said Ship and clandestinely unladed and run ashore within the Jurisdiction aforesaid between the said first day of March in the Year aforesaid and the Day of the Seizure aforesaid. Also for that Divers Goods and Commodities were unladed from the said Ship between the said first Day of March in the Year aforesaid and the Day of the Seizure aforesaid within the Jurisdiction aforesaid, before the said James Bartholomew then Master of the said Ship, had made known to the Governor of this Colony or the Person or Officer by him thereunto Authorized and appointed the arrival of the said Ship with her name and the name and Sirname of her Master and Commander and Shewn that She was an English Built Ship and navigated according to Law or had delivered to the said Governor or other Person or Officer a true and perfect Inventory and Invoice of her Lading together with the Place or Places in which the said Goods and Commodities were laden or taken into the said Ship, against the Forms

[9] The libel is endorsed with the reference "15 Chas. 2d.," presumably 15 Charles II, c. 7, *An Act for the Encouragement of Trade.* The act required that no European commodity should be imported into America unless it was loaded in England and shipped in a vessel built or owned in England, and manned by an English captain and a crew of whom three-quarters must be English. The act further required that an importer must give notice of his arrival within twenty-four hours, identify himself and his vessel, provide an inventory of cargo, and give proof that the vessel and crew were English as in the terms of the act; the importer must not unload his cargo until he had complied with these requirements, on pain of losing vessel, equipment, and cargo.

of the Statutes in such Cases made and provided by which the said Ship and her lading are forfeited one Moiety thereof to Our said Lord the King and the other Moiety to the said Hyde Parker who as well for our said Lord the King as for himself Prosecutes.[10]

Wherefore the said Hyde Parker prays the Advice of the Court in the Premisses.

The court condemned vessel and cargo. An advertisement in the *Virginia Gazette* (Purdie and Dixon) for April 30, 1772, announced the sale, to be held by decree of the court at Yorktown on May 4, of the *Jenifer* and a large quantity of gin in cases, barrels, and jugs, 500 stone and earthenware jugs, etc., evidently her cargo.

The next surviving court records, in order of date, are unique in the group, being a single sheet of what looks like the register's notes for inclusion in the court's proceedings on another case of alleged violation of the trade acts, the case of the sloop *Molly,* John White master, seized and libelled in July 1772 by William Maltby, commanding H.M.S. *Glasgow.*

The notes give the decree by which the *Molly* was condemned and forfeited, as follows:

From the Admiralty Court of Virginia

For that John White late Master of the Sloop Molly had imported into this Colony from Maryland a Quantity of Barr Iron having no Register or Clearance Adjudged 15 July 1772 that the said Sloop and her Lading be forfeited one Moiety to the King the other Moiety to the Prosecutor.

The notes also give this account of court costs: [11]

---

[10] The current regulations for distribution of the proceeds from sales of vessels and goods had been promulgated by an order in council of June 1, 1763 (P.R.O., P.C.2/110 pp. 23-25).

[11] It is not clear how the items of court costs were calculated. An instruction regarding fees charged for condemnation of a prize ship appeared in substantially the same form in all sets of instructions to the governors of Virginia from 1707 until the Revolution; the instruction directed that colonial courts of vice-admiralty were not to charge greater fees for condemnation of a prize than those taken in the High Court of Admiralty, amounting to about £10. For the instruction, and a list of fees taken in the High Court of Admiralty, see Leonard Woods Labaree, editor, *Royal Instructions to British Colonial Governors, 1670-1776* (New York, [1935]; reprinted New York, 1967), pp. 448-449. On March 5, 1771, President Nelson issued a notice (P.R.O., Adm.1/3884, unnumbered folio) repeating the instruction. A list of fees charged in the Virginia court in 1764 (P.R.O., C.O.325/5, unnumbered folio) states that the judge and other officers took a fee of £15 sterling for proceedings on a vessel of 100 tons or more, and of £10 sterling for proceedings on a smaller vessel. The marshal got a commission in sterling on the sale of a vessel or goods of 5 percent on the first £100 and 2½ percent on all over £100; he got fees in current money of ten shillings a day for traveling to arrest a vessel and of five shillings for arresting a vessel or citing a person. The register, presumably, took the fee of ten shillings current money for a copy of a decree. A list of fees taken in the court of vice-admiralty, sent with Fauquier's letter of May 20, 1767, to Shelburne, states that the judge and other officers of the court took £10 sterling for every court held, by act of Parliament. In 1768, John Randolph informed Lord Botetourt that the judge of vice-admiralty got £5 for each cause that came before him, and a memorial from Edward Montagu, the agent, of about 1769

By the Judge of the Court

The usual fees to the Officers of the Court	£12.10.—
Capt. Maltbys Attendance & travelling	6.—.—
One Officers Do.	3.—.—
Two Officers attendance on board the Sloop	6.10.—
The Appraisers	3.18.—
The Marshalls Account for travelling to Arrest and sell the Sloop &c	11.15. 6
The Register for Copies	2.—.—
	£45.13. 6

Other notes state the appraised value of the sloop as £550 and the proceeds of the sale as £366.10.9; the net value of the prize (the proceeds of the sale less the court costs) is given as £320.17.3, and the moiety of course as £160.8.7½, although neither net value nor moiety is identified as what it is. Finally, the notes mention William Maltby, presumably to identify him as the prosecutor, give the date of July 9, 1772, no doubt the date when the trial began, and add the memorandum "twenty tons of Barr Iron & Sloop Catharine." Probably "Catharine" is a slip of the pen for "Molly," as the sheet of notes is endorsed "Catharine" although it concerns the *Molly*.[12] The mention of iron is explained by the advertisement in the *Virginia Gazette* (Purdie and Dixon) for August 6, 1772, which announced the sale, on August 11, at Hampton, of the *Molly* and about twenty tons of iron in bars and ploughshares.

Ten days after the *Molly* was condemned, Maltby seized another sloop, the *Catharine*. Apparently the complete record of proceedings in the case has been preserved, as well as the file of miscellaneous documents related to the proceedings but not incorporated in them. The first document in the file is this citation, bearing the wafer seal of the court of vice-admiralty (the impression too faint to be visible), and signed by John Randolph:

[SEAL]

George the third by the Grace of God of Great Britain France and Ireland King

defined the fee as £5 Virginia currency (P.R.O., C.O.5/1347 ff. 52-53, 114-115). In a letter of March 17, 1771, Benjamin Waller gave the fee to the advocate for each court as £2.10.0 sterling, while a certificate of April 5, 1771, by Thomas Everard described the advocate's fees on prosecutions as £2.10.0 sterling for vessels of 100 tons or less, and £3.15.0 sterling for larger vessels (P.R.O., Adm.1/3884, two unnumbered folios). I have found no information on the other items of costs.

12 The notes are firmly identified with the *Molly* by William Maltby's "Remarks &ca. relative to a Tender being Purchas'd by Captain William Maltby," written in January 1775 after Maltby was tried by a court-martial. Maltby wrote that between June and December 1772 he took three vessels, which produced £202.19.11½ Virginia currency for the prosecutor, the largest prize being £160.8.7½. There had been an appeal by the owners of the vessel and cargo, and Maltby enclosed a copy of the court order of November 15, 1772, allowing an appeal by John White for the *Molly*. For Maltby's "Remarks" see P.R.O., Adm.1/2119, a long file of unnumbered documents concerning Maltby's court-martial.

Defender of the Faith &c. To John Tyler Marshall of our Court of vice Admiralty or his Deputy Greeting We command you that you arrest the Sloop Catharine whereof Peter Dilberg was late Master together with her Guns Rigging Tackle Apparel Furniture and her Lading and that you cite the said Master to appear before John Randolph Esqr. Commissary and Judge of our said Court at the Capitol in Williamsburg on Saturday the 1st Day of August next to answer William Maltby Esqr. Commander of our ship of War the Glasgow who as well for us as for himself prosecutes against the said sloop & her Lading. And have then there this Writ Witness the said John Randolph at Williamsburg the twenty eighth Day of July in the twelfth year of our Reign.

John Randolph

Following Randolph's signature is this deputation, dated July 30, 1772, and signed by John Tyler: "I depute Lewis Tyler to execute this Precept." Lewis Tyler was no doubt one of John Tyler's sons; he endorsed the citation as executed on July 30, 1772.

This is the record of proceedings in the case:

At a Court of Vice Admiralty held at the Cap[itol][13]
in Williamsburgh the 1st. day of August 1772

Before John Randolph Esqr. Commissary and Judge of the said Court

The Court was opened and James Hubard Gent produced a Commission to be Advocate of this Court in the room of Richard Starke decd. and he took the Oaths of Office.

And the Citation sued out of this Court by William Maltby Esqr. Commander of his Majestys Ship of War Glasgow against the Sloop Catharine whereof Peter Dilberg was late Master being returned by the Marshall Executed the said Peter Dilberg was called and not appearing the Advocate Exhibited a Libel against the said Sloop as follows[14]

Before you John Randolph Esq. commissary & Judge of the court of Viceadmiralty in the colony & dominion of Virginia

Cometh William Mal[t]by Esq. commander of his majesties ship of war the Glasgow (being duly authorized to make seizures) who as well for our lord the king as himself in this behalf prosecutes and gives this court to understand & be informed. That on the 25 day of July last past he seizd on the high sea within the Jurisdiction of this court the sloop Catharine whereof Peter Dilberg was then master with all her guns tackle apparel and furniture, and also 5 hhds. & 2 barrells of rum or spirits one hhd. of sugar & one hhd molasses the lading of the said sloop Catharine for that within the first day of July last past & the day of the seizure of the aforesaid sloop & lading the said rum or spirits & the said sugar & molasses were imported or brought into this colony in the said sloop, without the master of the said sloop having produced to the Governour of this colony or the proper officer by him appointed for that

[13] A corner of the page is torn off here.
[14] MS has "(here enter it)," the libel being a separate document.

purpose a certificate according to the act of Parliament in that case made & provided, shewing that the said sloop is qualifyd to trade here according to the said act, or having a certificate & clearance shewing the place of the growth produce or manufacture of the spirits sugar & molasses as requird by the acts of Parliament in those cases made & provided by which means the said sloop with her guns tackel apparel & furniture, & the said 5 hhds & 2 barrels of spirits, & the said sugars & molasses are forfeited, one moiety to our said lord the king, the other to the said William Mal[t]by Esq, who prosecutes as well four our said lord the king as himself Wherefore the said William Mal[t]by prays the advice of the court in the premises, &c.

Whereupon the usual Proclamation was made and no Person appearing to Claim the said Sloop the Court was adjourned til Monday next 6 oClock in the afternoon.

3d. August 1772

Present John Randolph Esqr.

The Court was opened and the usual Proclamation was again made the said Dilberg appeared and Confessed [th]e Allegations of the Libel to be true Decree that the said Sloop and her Lading be Condemned and forfeited one Moiety to the King the other Moiety to the Libellant and It is Ordered that the said Sloop and her Lading be Appraised by George Wray John Jones and Henry King or any 2 of them they being first Sworn for that purpose that the Marshal make Sale of the said Sloop and her Lading at Public Auction for ready Money and return the Appraisment and Sales to the Court on Saturday the 15th. Instant.[15]

15 August 1772.

Present John Randolph Esqr.

The Court was opened and an Appraisment of the said Sloop and her Lading was returned and is as follows[16]

An Appraisment of Sloop Catharine & her Cargo vizt.

Sloop, Furniture &c			£ 30.—.—
5 hhds New York Rum quantity	513 Galls.	@ 2/ per Galln.	51. 6.—
2 Casks Whiskey	51 do.	1/6	3:16: 6
1 hhd Molosses	107 do.	1/6	8. 0. 6
1 hhd Brown Sugar Quantity	900 li Net	@ 37/6 per Cwt.	16.17. 6
			£110: 0: 6

In Compliance to an Order of the Court of Vice Admiralty dated 3d. Instant, We the Subscribers being first Sworn have Appraised the Sloop Catharine &c as above

Given under our hands this 11th. August 1772

George Wray
H: King
Jno. Jones

---

15 The *Virginia Gazette* (Purdie and Dixon) for August 6, 1772, advertised the sale, on August 11, at Hampton, of the sloop *Catharine*, 5 hogsheads and 2 barrels of rum, 1 hogshead of molasses, and 1 hogshead of brown sugar.

16 MS has "(here enter it)," the appraisal being a separate document.

Also an Account of the Sales thereof Vizt.[17]

The Sales of the Sloop Catharine & Cargoe, August 11th. 1772.	
Mr. Salkeld 3 Hogds Rum 317 Galls. @ 2/	£ 31.14. 0
Mr. Miles King 2 Do. @ 1/10½ 196 Galls.	18. 7. 6
Captn. King 2 Casks of Whiskey 57 Galls. @ 1/3½	3. 5.10½
Mr. Jacob Wray 1 Hogd. Molosses 107 Galls. @ 1/5d	7. 9. 7
Captn. King 1 Hogd of White Sugar 900 lbs. @ 32/6d	14.12. 6
The Sloop & Furniture to Mr. Blake	30. 0. 0
	£105. 9. 5½
Marshall's Commission deducted	5. 2. 9
	£100. 6. 8½

The Court then Examined the Charges and Expences arising upon the Seizure and a Mariners Wages and allowed for the same £36.19.— which being deducted from the said Sales leaves a balance of £63.7.8. Whereupon it is Decreed and Ordered that the Marshall pay to Cary Michell Esqr. Collector of his Majestys Customs at Hampton £31.13.10 a Moiety of the aforesaid balance and to the Libell[ant] £31.13.10 the other Moiety thereof.

Charges allowed

Fees of the Court	£12.10
Two Officers for Attendance	3.—
Charles Boush a Witness	4.17
Marshalls Account	10. 5
Appraisers	2. 2
Register for Copies	1.—
Robert Thornton a Mariner his Wages	3. 5
	£36.19

In addition to the citation and proceedings of the court, the file on the case of Maltby vs. the sloop *Catharine* includes the order for appraisal and sale noted in the proceedings of August 3, 1772, and five accounts corresponding to as many items in the charges allowed by the court. These are the order and accounts:

[A. Order for appraisal and sale of the *Catharine*.]

At a Court of Vice Admiralty held at the Capitol
in Williamsburgh the 3d. day of August 1772.

Ordered

That George Wray, John Jones & Henry King being first sworn before a Justice of the Peace do Appraise in Current Money the Sloop Catherine together with her Rigging Tackle Apparel and Furniture and her Lading and that the Marshall of this Court after Public Notice given make Sale of the said Sloop and her Lading at

[17] MS has "(here enter it)," the account being a separate document. Presumably "white sugar" should be "brown sugar."

A[u]ction for ready Money and return the Appraisment with an Account of the Sales to the Court on Saturday the 15th of this Instant.

THOS. EVERARD Register

On the back of the order is the address "For Mr. Tyler," and the endorsement "Eliza. City sc George Wray, John Jones & Henry King were Sworn before me Augt. 11th. 1772. WA: MCCLURG."

[B. Prosecutor's account.]

1772	The Sloop Catharine	
	To the Glasgow	
	The Master's Attending 4 days	2. 0. 0
	The Clerk 2 Do	1. 0. 0
		£3. 0. 0

[C. Witness's account.]

Sloop Catharine to Charles Boush	Dr.
To travelling from Norfolk to Williamsburgh once and from Hampton Road twice and three days Attendance	£4.17.—

CHAS BOUSH

[D. Marshal's account.]

72	The Sloop Catharine	Dr
July 29th	Traveling to Hampton Road	2. 5. 0
	Citing & Arresting	0.10. 0
	Boat hire to Hamn. Road & Attending	0. 7. 6
	Summoning two Witnesses	0.10. 0
Augt.	Traveling to Hampton	2. 0. 0
	Summoning the Appraisers & giving notice to a Justice to Swear them	1. 0. [0][18]
	Attending Do	1. 0. [0]
	one days attendance Taking out the Cargoe	0.10. [0]
	Advertising the Vessel & Cargoe	0. 3. [0]
	Punch at the Sale	1. 0. [0]
	Attending the Court	1. 0. [0]
		£10. 5. 6

J TYLER Marshal

[E. Appraisers' account.]

The Sloop Catharine	Dr.
1772	
Augt. 11 To appraising said Sloop & Cargo @ 14/ each	£2.2.—

GEO WRAY
JNO. JONES
HENRY KING

[18] From this point the pence column has been torn off, except for the total.

[F. Mariner's account.]

Sloop Catharine to Robert Thornton	Dr.
For Pay Due from the 4th. of June to the	£ s d
3 of August 1772, @ 32/6 per Month	3. 5. 0
Peter Dilberg	his
	ROBERT X THORNTON
	Mark

On the back of the account is the endorsement "James City Sc August 3d. 1772 Robt. Thornton made Oath that the within Account is Just & True J Tyler," and the note "Recd. £1.10.—," presumably made by Tyler as a justice of the peace for James City County and recording payment of a fee for administering the oath.

Early in September, presumably, Maltby seized a cutter called the *Generous Friend* or *Generous Friends*. On September 10, Randolph heard the case and dismissed the cutter on payment of costs. In a letter of December 24, 1772, to the Customs Commissioners at Boston, Captain Maltby observed of this case "The Judge has likewise thought proper to clear a Cutter that I had Seiz'd who pretended he came from England in Ballast with Letters for this Colony, She had neither Register or any kind of Clearance whatever, I also add a Copy of the Marshalls Letter relative to the said Cutter."[19] Tyler's letter to Maltby, September 10, 1772, reported that the case of the *Generous Friends* had been heard that day, and the cutter acquitted upon payment of costs. Tyler enclosed this account, tendered on Maltby's request but not allowed by the judge:

1772	The Cutter Generous Friends to William Maltby	Dr
	To the Master of Midshipmen attending 7 days each coming up from Hampton Road	7. 0. 0
	Horse hire twice to Williamsburg	0. 7. 6
	15 days attendance an Officer to take care of the Cutter	2. 5.—

At the end of the following week in September, Randolph heard another ordinary maritime case. It seems that these are all of the records in the case:

At a Court of Vice Admiralty held at the
Capitol the 19th. day of Sept. 1772
Before John Randolph Esqr. Commissary and Judge

The Court was opened and the Citation sued out of the said Court by David Wilkins against the Ship Union whereof Charles Poole is Master being returned by

[19] Maltby's letter and its enclosures are in P.R.O., T.1/501 f. 355. The *Virginia Gazette* (Purdie and Dixon) for September 10, 1772, reported that the *Generous Friend,* Captain Smith, sent express from London to the merchants in Virginia "on Account of the late Failures," had been seized by the *Glasgow* for want of a register, but was discharged on September 10 by the court of admiralty, with payment of costs.

the Marshal Executed James Hubard Advocate Exhibited a Libel which is as followeth[20]

Before you John Randolph Esq commissary & Judge of the court of vice admiralty in the colony & dominion of Virginia

Cometh David Wilkins second mate of the ship Union whereof Charles Poole is master & against the said ship he doth alledge as [follows]

Imprimis He doth article alledge & propound that by the marine laws all ships & vessels are liable for mariners wages earn'd & perfo[rm]ed.

Item That on the 24 of August 1771 he saild from the port of Leverpool in Great Brittain in the said ship Union on a voyage to Africa as second mate thereof at the rate of £3.10 Sterling per month, & that by the custom of the African trade, & particular agreement between the libellant & the said Poole it was stipulated that a moiety of all wages due shoud be paid in the country where the slaves were sold.

Item That some time about the fifth of August 1772 the said ship arrived in this colony with a cargoe of slaves, upon the sale of which the libellant with the rest of the mariners became entitled to a moiety of their wages.[21]

Item That on the libellants demanding his wages as to a moiety the said Poole was displeasd with him & in consequence thereof dismissd him from his office, & then orderd him to leave the ship & recover his wages as he coud, the first mate being orderd to see that he had none of the ships provisions from that time, & the mariners on board not to obey him as an officer.

Item That the amount of the wages due to him is £43.5.7½ currency. Wherefore he prays that the said ship may be made liable for the said wages.

And the said Charles Poole by Ben Waller Proctor in this Court appeared and put in his Answer which is as follows[22]

The Answer of Charles Pole Master of the Ship or Vessel called the Union to the Libel of David Wilkins exhibited against him and the said Ship

This Respondent doth admit the first Article in the said Libel but with such Restrictions as by Law and the Articles signed by himself and the Crew of the said Ship for the Voiage which he brings into Court and refers to, is provided.

He also admits the second Article in the said Libel except that by the Articles aforesaid the Mariners Wages were to be paid Currency for Sterling as will appear by the said Articles.

He admits the third Article in the said Libel but submits to the Court on Consideration of his Answer and Proofs whether the Libellant is intitled to any Wages at all.

To the fourth Article he saith that frequently during their Voiage the Libellant would quit the said Ship in the Night leaving no other Officer on Board and go on board other Vessels and return in Liquor in the Morning and would frequently in the Absence of this Respondent and the first Mate when the Ship was under his

---

20 MS has "(here enter it)," the libel being a separate document.

21 The *Virginia Gazette* (Purdie and Dixon) for August 20, 1772, announced the sale on August 26, at Osborne's on James River, of about 280 "fine healthy Gold Coast Slaves," just arrived from Africa in the ship *Union*.

22 MS has "(here enter it)," the answer being a separate document.

Care be drunk for Days together and on the Coast of Africa embezzled some of the Cargo of Tobacco and on the Voyage some of the Ships Liquors that whilst the Ship lay at Osborne's in this Colony in the Absence of this Respondent the Libellant stripped himself seized and offerred Violence to the Chief Mate which was the Cause this Respondent removed the Libellant from his Office of second Mate and treated him as a Common Mariner and upon the Complaint of the Chief Mate that the Libellant had got drunk and threatened to throw the Carpenter over Board this Respondent discharged the Libellant from the ship thinking he had a Right so to do after such mutinous and outragious Behaviour wherefore he prays to be hence dismissed with his Reasonable Costs and that the said Ship may be discharged from her Arrest.

CHARLES POLE

Sworn to in Court
19 Sept. 1772.

To which the Advocate replied Generally whereupon divers Witnesses were Sworn and Examined Viva Voce in Court and the Cause being heard on the Libel and Answer the Evidence aforesaid and the Arguments of the Counsel on both sides Decree that the Respondent [p]ay[23] the Libellant £26.18.4 Current Money as the balance due of his Wages and that the Costs be paid Equally by the Parties.

Usual fees of the Court	£12.10.—
Marshals Account	2.16. 3
Respondents Council	5.—.—
	£20. 6. 3

One half to be paid by the Libellant
the other half by the Respondent.

JOHN RANDOLPH

This itemized account from the marshal accompanies other papers in the case:

1772	The Ship Union	Dr
Sepr 18th	Traveling Citing & Arresting	1. 5. 0
	Ferriages	1. 3
	Attending the Court	1. 0. 0
		£2. 6. 3
	Summoning two Witnesses	0.10. 0
		£2.16. 3

J. TYLER Marshal

The next surviving record from the vice-admiralty court is an order allowing an appeal from the court's decree of July 15, 1772, condemning the

[23] The first letter is obliterated.

sloop *Molly*. This order is not among the Webb-Prentis Papers, but in the Treasury Papers at the Public Record Office, London, as an enclosure in a letter of January 22, 1773, from the Commissioners of the Customs, Boston, to the Treasury (P.R.O., T.1/501 f. 358).[24] The order is as follows:

At a Court of Vice Admiralty held at the Capitol in Williamsburg the 25th day of November 1772 Before John Randolph Esqr. Commissary and Judge of the said Court.

Upon a Motion made to the Court on behalf of the Owners of the Sloop Molly (whereof John White was late Master) Condemned by the Decree of this Court the 15th. day of July last as forfeited from which Decree the said Master had prayed an Appeal to the High Court of Admiralty of Great Britain which was to be allow'd on his giving Security on or before the 25th of the same Month but he failing so to do. It is now Ordered by the Court that the Appeal aforesaid be allowed Security being this Day given to Prosecute the same, and it is further Order'd that the Owners aforesaid or their Agent give Notice thereof to Captain William Maltby the Libellant.

Signed/ Thomas Everard Register

A Copy

This order of the court evoked representations to the Commissioners in Boston from officers of the Customs in Virginia and from Captain Maltby as well, forwarded in January 1773 to the Treasury. The correspondence is in P.R.O., T.1/501 ff. 354-360. On December 5, 1772, Cary Michell, Collector, and Samuel Allyne, Comptroller, wrote from the Lower District of James River to the Commissioners to transmit a copy of the order, which they described as "an unprecedented proceeding, and tending to the Discouragement of Officers making Seizures." On December 24, Captain Maltby sent a copy of the order to the Commissioners, and wrote this about it:

A very odd and unexpected appeal has been allowed here of which Inclosed you have a Copy, the Vessel mentioned therein being about 35 or 40 Tons with 20 Ton of Iron from Maryland to this Colony having neither Register or any kind of clearance whatever. She was forfeited as you will observe in the copy of the allow'd appeal, Condemn'd, Sold &ca. and the Money arrising from the Sale devided by the Order of the Judge of said Court of Vice Admiralty agreable to His Majesty's Proclamation in that behalf. It is certainly very extraordinary that an appeal should be allow'd Four Months after Condemnation, Sale and Distribution of the Money.

Maltby added his comment on the dismissal of the *Generous Friends,* cited above, and concluded with the postscript "how farr the Judge has acted

[24] Two more copies of the order are in P.R.O., Adm.1/2119, among other papers (with no page or folio numbers) concerning a court-martial held on Captain William Maltby.

right &ca. in his proceedings in these Cases, I must refer to you and beg your Opinion on the matter."

It appears that the appeal on the *Molly* was not made after all, or in any case no mention of such an appeal has been found in the Admiralty records in the Public Record Office. Captain Maltby referred to the appeal in his "Remarks," written in January 1775,[25] where he observed that he did not know whether the appeal had been settled; he would no doubt have been notified, as libellant, of the disposition of the appeal.

Towards the end of 1772, presumably, Randolph heard the last ordinary maritime case represented in the Webb-Prentis Papers. The one surviving record of the case is this libel:

> Before you John Randolph Esq commissary & Judge of the court of vice admiralty in the colony & dominion of Virginia
>
> Cometh John Welch owner of the sloop Patty whereof Joseph Basden was late master & against the ship Peters whereof Thomas Lang is master doth article propound alledge & declare as follows
>
> Imprimis He doth alledge & declare that by the ma[r]ine law, every ship or vessell together with her rigging apparel & furniture which shall under sail or under the command of her sails run foul of, strike against or grapple with another, that is not under the full command of her sails, shall be obliged & is liable to make full & compleat satisfaction for all damages accruing to the vessel run or struck against.
>
> Item that the said sloop Patty on the 7 day of Septr. last being then in good order & repair & having on board a considerable quantity of money & valuable merchandize saild from the island of St Christophers on a voyage to Philadelphia & on the 25 of the said month in the Lat. of 36°51′ & about 5 leagues distant from cape Charles met with a violent gale of wind, which broke & tore her Jibb sail to peices.
>
> Item That on the 26 of the said month about 6 of the clock in the morning the wind blowing very hard at ENE, & the sloop Patty being close hauld under her mainsail & foresail in order to keep off the shore, the ship Peter was observed to Windward, bearing down directly upon her, with the wind at large, as if to speak her.
>
> Item That the said ship Peters, on the said 26 day of Septr on the high seas & within the Jurisdiction of this court did carelessly negligently & designedly run foul of, strike against & grapple with the said sloop Patty, & thereby did so damage & injure the said sloop, that the master & crew expecting she was foundering did with great difficulty & for preservation of their lives desert the said sloop & get into the said ship Peters, but that they were obliged to leave on board the said sloop two negroe boys & all the money & merchandize to the mercy of the waves, the said Thomas Lang master of the said ship refusing to lie by or to give them any assistance to recover & secure their vessel & property, thus lost to them thro his fault & negligence, & that the said ship Peters with the master & crew of the said sloop on the same day & in a few hours after the damage done, did arrive in this colony.

[25] See note 12 above.

Item that the said John Welch thro the negligence of the said Thomas Lang has sustaind damage to the value of five thousand pounds wherefore he prays the advice of the court in the premisses & that the said ship with her tackle &c may be condemnd to make full restitution for the same.[26]

Nothing is known of the outcome of Welch's suit. Evidently the *Peters* was not condemned, for no advertisement of the sale of the ship was published in the *Virginia Gazette.*

The records of the next case, one involving an alleged violation of the trade acts, are complete except for the marshal's account of sales of a flat, or flatboat, and its cargo. These are the proceedings:

At a Court of Vice Admiralty held at the Capitol in Williamsburgh on Tuesday the 7th. day of Decr. 1773 and in the fourteenth Year of the Reign of our Sovereign Lord King George the third

Before John Randolph Esqr. Commissary and Judge of the said Court

The Court was opened and the Citation sued out by Tyringham Howe Esqr. Commander of his Majestys Sloop Cruiser against a Flatt and 15 Pipes of Wine being by the Marshal returned that he had Arrested the said Flatt and Wine but the Master not being to be found a Copy of the Citation was affixed on the said Flatt.

Whereupon James Hubard Advocate Exhibited a Libell which is as follows[27]

Before you John Randolph Esq commissary & Judge of the court of Vice Admiralty in the colony & dominion of Virginia cometh Tyringham Howe commander of his majesties sloop of war the Cruiser, who is duly authorised to make seizures, & prosecutes now as well for our lord the king as himself, & gives the court to understand & be informd that on the 20th. day of November in the year of our lord 1773 at the port of Hampton on the high seas & within the Jurisdiction of this court he seizd a vessel commonly calld a Flat, the property of some person unkno[wn] together with fifteen pipes of wine which were laden on board the said vessel or flatt, because that the said 15 pipes of wine were laden on board the said vessel or flatt to be landed & put on shore, before the duties thereon were paid or secured to be paid to the proper officer for that purpose appointed, as is by law required, & because that the said vessel or flatt was aiding and assisting in the landing & putting on shore the said 15 pipes [of] wine, by means whereof the said 15 pipes of wine

---

[26] The *Virginia Gazette* (Purdie and Dixon) for October 1, 1772, had an account of the collision between the *Peter,* Captain Lang, from Glasgow, and the sloop *Patty,* identified only as a sloop from St. Christopher's bound to Philadelphia; Lang thought it unsafe to put about for the sloop on account of the high sea and strong wind. The newspaper account mentioned the two Negro boys, a cargo of West India produce not further identified, and 800 Half Joes, Portuguese gold coins worth about £1,440 sterling. The account further mentioned that the *Patty,* according to her master's statement, had still been at St. Christopher's on the last day of August, although no record of her clearance has been found. The naval officer's list for St. Christopher's (P.R.O., T.1/493 f. 33) records that the *Patty* was entered on August 7, 1772, the property of Joseph Welch and registered at Basseterre. If Welch was a resident of the Leeward Islands, he may not have had time to file his suit until some date in 1773.

[27] MS has "(here Enter it)," the libel being a separate document.

together with the said vessel or flat are forfeited, one moiety thereof to our said lord the other to the said Tyringham Howe. Wherefore the said Tyringha[m] Howe prays the advice of the court in the premisses, & that the said vessel or flat together with the 15 pipes of wine may be condemnd & forfeited as before set forth.

The Usual Proclamation was then made and no Person appearing to Claim the said Flatt or the said Wine the Court adjourned til Tomorrow 12 oClock.

8th. Decr. 1773

Present J. Randolph Esqr.

The Court was opened and Proclamation being again made and no Person appearing to Claim the said Flatt or Wine the Court was then Adjourned til Tomorrow Morning 11 oClock.

9 Decr. 1773 Present J. Randolph Esqr

The Court was opened and the usual Proclamation was again made and no Person appearing to Claim the said Flatt or Wine the said Libel is taken as true and It is thereupon Adjudged and Decreed by the Court that the said Flatt and Wine be Condemned and forfeited One Moiety to our Sovereign Lord the King and the other Moiety to Tyringham Howe Esqr. the Prosecutor. and It is Ordered that the Marshall make Sale of the said Flatt and Wine at A[u]ction for ready Money he having the same first appraised by [ ] [28] who are to be Sworn before a Magistrate for that purpose and return the Appraisment with an Account of the Sales to the Court on Thursday the 23d. of this Instant and then the Court adjourned til Thursday the 23d. of this Instant December.

23 Decr. 1773.

Present John Randolph Esqr. Commissary and Judge

The Court was opened and the Marshal returned an Account of Sales of the said Flatt and Wines as follows (here enter it)[29] the Court then Examined the Accounts of the Expences attending the Seizure with the Court Charges and allowed for the same £50.12.6 which being deducted from the said Sales leaves a balance of £151.7.8.

Whereupon it is Ordered that the Marshall after paying of the said Charges pay £75.13.10 a Moiety of the said balance to Cary Michell Esqr. Collector of his Majestys Customs at Hampton for the Use of his Majesty and £75.13.10 the other Moiety thereof to the said Tyringham Howe the Prosecutor.

The fees of the Court	£12.10.—
The Prosecutors Account	15. 6.—
The Marshalls [Account] [30]	15. 7. 6
James Atherton Cryer of the Court	1.—.—
The Registers Account	3.—.—
	£47. 3. 6

John Randolph

[28] MS has a blank space, about two thirds of a line.

[29] The account is missing. The *Virginia Gazette* (Rind) for December 9, 1773, advertised the sale, to take place on December 17, at Gosport, of a flat and fifteen pipes of wine.

[30] Hole in MS.

Joseph Calvert a Witness omitted	3. 9.—
	50.12. 6

The last of the cases among the surviving records of the court of vice-admiralty is again one involving alleged violations of the trade acts. It stands out among the other cases because of its length, the variety of documents included, the libelling of two vessels, and the allowing of appeals to the High Court of Admiralty from both libellant and respondent:

Virginia.

At a Court of Vice Admiralty held at the Capitol in Williamsburgh the 25th. day of March 1775 and in the fifteenth Year of the Reign of our Sovereign Lord George the third by the Grace of God of Great Britain France and Ireland King Defender of the faith &c

Before J[oh]n [31] Randolph Esqr. Commissary and Judge of the said Court

The Court was opened and the Citation sued out of the said Court by Henry Collins Esqr. Commander of his Majestys Sloop of War the Magdalen against the Sloop Liberty (whereof Stephen a Negro Slave late was Master) and her Lading being by the Marshal returned "Executed" the Court adjourned til Tuesday the 28th. Instant.

28 March 1775

Present John Randolph Esqr.

James Hubbard Esqr the Advocate exhibited a Libel against the said Sloop Liberty and her Lading which Libel is as follows to wit [32]

Before you John Randolph Esq commissary & judge of the court of viceadmiralty in the colony & dominion of Virginia Cometh Henry Collins Esq commander of his majesties sloop of war Magdalen who's duly authorised to make seizures & who now prosecutes as well for our lord the King as himself & gives the court to understand & be informd that on the 14 day [of] March in the year of our lord 1775 in the port of Williamsburg in this colony on the high seas & within the jurisdiction of this court he seizd the sloop Liberty whereof a negroe slave named Stephen was late skipper together with her guns tackle rigging apparel furniture boats & lading consisting of 16 hhds. containing [ ] [33] gallons of rum or spirits, 200 lb of coffee, 100 lb of chocolate & 1000 bushells of oats & four negroe slaves for that viz *that* between the day of seizure aforesaid & the first day of January in the year aforesaid the aforesaid goods & lading were laden & put on board the said sloop Liberty in the port of Accomack without a sufferance first had & obtaind from the proper officer for that purpose appointed contrary to the form of the statute in that case made & provided for that viz *that* the said 16 hhds containing [ ] gallons of foreign rum or spirits & not rum or spirits of the growth produce or manufacture of any brittish

[31] Hole in MS.

[32] MS has "(here enter it)," the libel being a separate document.

[33] Here and below the MS has a blank space before "gallons." The marshal's account of marks and numbers on the hogsheads, just after the proceedings, indicates that the hogsheads contained about 1,930 gallons.

colony or plantation in America were imported sometime between the day of seizure aforesaid & the first day of January in the year aforesaid in the sloop Betsy whereof Stephen Sampson was master into the port of Accomack in this colony & unladed & put aboard the said sloop Liberty secretly & fraudulent[l]y to be removed & carried away contrary to the acts of trade in that [case made & provided] [34] for that viz *that* th[e said 16 hhds] [35] containing [ ] gallons of rum or spirits were imported into this colony in the said Betsy whereof Stephen Sampson was master sometime between the day of seizure aforesaid & the first day of January in the year aforesaid & unladed & discharged therefrom before the master thereof had been to the proper officer for that purpose appointed & made a true & faithfull entry & report of his vessel & her lading & produced to him the proper certificates proving the place of the growth produce or manufacture of the said rum or spirits contrary to the acts of trade in those cases made & provided for that viz *that* the said 16 hhds containing [ ] gallons of rum or spirits were laden on board the said sloop Betsy before bond was given that the said rum or spirits nor any part thereof shoud be unladed in the isle of man contrary to the form of the statute in that case made & provided for that viz *that* the said 200 lb of coffee sometime between the day of seizure aforesaid & the first day of January in the year aforesaid were imported into this colony in the said sloop Betsy whereof Stephen Sampson was master & unladed & put ashore as merchandize before the duties or customs due thereon were paid to the proper officer for that purpose appointed & before he had produced to the proper officer a certificate of his having given bond for the due unlading of the same as the acts of trade in that [case] made require, & made a true & faithfull report of his vessel's arrival & her lading for that viz that the said sloop Liberty with her guns &c was aiding & assisting & imployd privately to remove the said 16 hhds of rum or spirits containing [ ] gallons & the said 200 lb of coffee from the said sloop Betsy contrary to the form of the statute in that case made & provided *By means* whereof the said sloop Liberty with her guns &c. & her lading aforesaid are liable to be forfeited & divided one moiety thereof to our sovereign lord the King the other to the said Henry Collins who prosecutes on this occasion. Wherefore he prays the advice of the court in the premisses & that the said sloop Liberty with her guns &c. & her lading &c may be forfeited [cond]emnd [36] & divided as above.

And Thorowgood Smith with sufficient security having given Bond for Costs according to the directions of the Act of Parliament made in the fourth year of his present Majestys Reign [37] time is given him and the rest of the Owners of the said Sloop and her Lading til the 30th Instant to put in their Claim and Answer [to] the said Libel and the Court Adjourned til the 30th. Instant.

30 March 1775.

Present John Randolph Esqr

Further time is given the Respondents til the 1st. day of April next to put in their Claim & Answer Then the Court adjourned til the 1st day of April next.

[34] Hole in MS.

[35] Hole in MS.

[36] Hole in MS.

[37] Probably 4 Geo. III, c. 15, *An Act for granting certain Duties . . . in America . . .*, which provided that no person could enter a claim until he had given security of £60 for costs.

1st. April 1775

Present John Randolph Esqr.

On the Motion of the Respondents by George Wythe Esqr. a Proctor of this Court It is Ordered that the Libellant file with the Register of the Court the Certificate said to be granted by Littleton Savage for the sixteen hhds of Rum mentioned in the Libel that the Marshal go on board the said Sloop Liberty and take an Account of the Marks and Numbers of the said Hogsheads and report the same to the Court[38] that the Libellant put into the care of the Marshal the Respondents Apprentice named Elligood Ayres who is to be examined as a Witness and that the said Marshal do not suffer any Person to interrogate the said Witness until his examination in Court and further time is given the Respondents til the 3d. Instant to put in their Claim and Answer and then the Court adjourned til the 3d. of this Instant.

3d. April 1775.

Present John Randolph Esqr.

The Respondents put in their Claim and Answer which is as follows[39]

Before you John Randolph esquire commissary and judge of the court of vice admirality in the colony and dominion of Virginia come John Bowdoin Isaac Smith and Preeson Bowdoin Merchants by their proctor and Thorowgood Smith merchant in his proper person the said John Bowdoin and Isaac Smith being owners of the sloop Liberty and executors of the last will and testament of Severn Eyre esquire deceased who was owner of a negro slave named Stephen late skipper of the said sloop Liberty and the said John Bowdoin being owner of two other negro slaves one hundred and sixty five pounds weight of coffee and forty pounds weight of chocolate on board the said sloop Liberty and the said Thorowgood Smith John Bowdoin and Preeson Bowdoin being owners of sixteen hogsheads of rum or spirits and one thousand bushels of oats on board the said sloop Liberty and respectively claim the said sloop Liberty slaves rum or spirits coffee chocolate and oats seised by Henry Collins esquire commander of his majesty's sloop of war Magdalen, and not confessing or acknowledging the said Henry Collins to be duly authorized to make seizures in any river where the said sloop was seized and not on the high seas and saving and reserving to themselves all advantages of exception to the imperfections of the libel exhibited in this court by the said Henry Collins in order to condemn the said sloop Liberty and her loading as forfeited for answer to the said libel or to so much thereof as they are advised it is material for them to make answer unto make answer and say, that the said slaves were the watermen who were put on board the said sloop not as any part of her cargo or lading but only to navigate her from Hungars in the county of Northampton to Chesterhill in the county of Chesterfield on James river and there to deliver the said rum or spirits and coffee chocolate and oats to one Thomas Randolph merchant to whom they were consigned and these respondents are advised and do insist that the loading the said goods on board the said sloop Liberty without a sufferance first had from an officer was not contrary to the form of any statute and that the said sloop which was proceeding with her said loading

[38] The account was duly made, and follows after the proceedings, below. The proceedings do not indicate that the account was reported to the court.

[39] MS has "(here enter it)," the claim and answer being a separate document.

directly to her aforesaid place of destination was not liable to seizure and these respondents not being able to declare of their own knowledge that the said rum or spirits is of the produce or manufacture of any of the colonies or plantations in America in the possession or under the dominion of his majesty do refer to a certificate under the hands and seals of the officers of the customs of the port of Accomack hereunto annexed and submit the same to the judgment of this court as a proof that the sixteen hogsheads of rum in the libel mentioned are part of the rum mentioned in the said certificate the marks numbers and contents of the one agreeing with those of the other and hope such proof will appear sufficient and satisfactory it being impossible for them to adduce any other evidence of a product or manufacture of one of the british American iles and these respondents denying that the said sixteen hogsheads of rum or spirits were unladed and put on board the said sloop Liberty secretly and fraudulently to be removed and carried away to prove the contrary in some measure refer to the certificate of the affidavit made by Stephen Sampson in the libel named which as the respondents believe is in the hands or custody of the libellant and which they pray that he may be required to produce that the said liquors had been duly entered and duties thereof secured. And as to the allegations in the libel that the said sixteen hogsheads of rum or spirits were imported into this colony in the sloop Betsey whereof Stephen Sampson was master since the first day of January last and unladed and discharged therefrom before the master thereof had been to the proper officer for that purpose appointed and made a true and faithful entry and report of his vessel and her lading and produced to him the proper certificates and were laden aboard the sloop Betsy before bond was given that the said rum or spirits should not be unladed in the Isle of Man these respondents for answer thereto refer to the foregoing part of this their answer and the certificate of the custom-house officers there mentioned. and these respondents further say they hope to make it appear that the coffee on board the said sloop Liberty was imported into this colony not in the said sloop Betsy but in the schooner Wray-galley and that the same was properly entered and the duty for it paid And these respondents denying that the said sloop liberty with her guns was as the libel suggests aiding and assisting and employed privately to remove the said sixteen hogsheads of rum or spirits and any coffee whatever from the said sloop Betsy pray to be hence dismissed with their costs.

The Certificates refered to in this Answer is as follow [40]

Port of Accomack }
Virginia }

These are to Certifye all whom it may Concern that John Bowdoin Thorowgood Smith & Co: have at sundry times within Twelve Months from this Date Imported into this Port the Following Quantity of Rum as Appears by the Original Papers & our Books.

---

[40] At the end of the claim and answer above, in the same hand as the proceedings, is this line and "(here Enter Certificates marked A.B.)."

T 4 S

No 1 to 22 hhds.

viz. on the 20th: of June 1774 In the Betsey Stephen Sampson Twenty two hogsheads from St Christophers

No. 1 to 6 S.S.
from 6 to 14 T 4 S hhds:

On the 20th July 1774 fourteen hhds: per the Squirrel Daniel Sturgis from Nevis

B.E.S. No: 1 a 2 hhds
T 4 S No: 1 to 46 do.
do 1 Tierce.
do No: 1 to 21 Bls.

On the 2nd: November forty eight hhds, one tierce & Twenty one Barrels from Antigua in the Betsey Stephen Sampson.

The Duty on which Rum were legally secured with the Naval Officer on the Entry thereof according to Law. Given under our hands & Seals of Office at the Custom-House the 20th: March 1775.

Walter Hatton Collector
D. Bowman Naval Officer
Francis Miller Comptroller

Northampton
County Sct.

T 4 S

No. 10. 4. 22
11. 13. 8. 14
9. 11. 8. 6. 5
12. 3. 9. 1.

Stephen Sampson made oath before me one of his Majestys Justices of the peace for the County aforesaid that Sixteen Hhds Rum now on board the sloop Liberty Negro Stephen Skipper was legally imported in the Sloop Betsey and the duties secured According to Act of Assembly, being marked & Numberd as per Margin Certified under my Hand this Tenth Day of March 1775.

Litt: Savage

and the Libellant Replied thereto Generally whereupon Elligood Ayres was produced to be examined as a Witness to which the Respondents objected alledging that the said Ayres was impressed into his Majestys Service on board the Magdalen and in Case of a Condemnation of the said Sloop & Lading would be intitled to a part thereof but the Libellant declaring in Court that the said Witness was free and discharged from any Impress the said Objection is Overruled. The Court then Examined the said Ayres and John Bowdoin as Witnesses whose Depositions are as follow [41]

[41] MS has "(here enter them Ayres first and then Bowdoin's)," the two depositions constituting a separate document, in which Bowdoin's deposition comes first.

Elligood Ayres Mariner belonging to the Sloop Betsey an Apprentice to Mr. Thorowgood Smith & Co. aged upwards of eighteen Years being sworn saith That he has Served as an Apprentice between 4 and 5 Years that a short time before Ch[r]is[t]-mas last the said Sloop Sailed from Hungars to St Eustatia and returned from thence to this Colony without touching at any other Place that there were taken on board the said Sloop at St. Eustatia 40 hhds of Rum or Spirits eight Hhds of Molasses 8 Cases of Gin 36 Cags of Brandy 14 Boxes of Claret about 100 Weight of Coffee in an Oznabrigs bag and brought the same on board the Betsey into Hungars in this Colony that the said Rum and Brandy were put into Mr. Bowdoins Store house and that John Read of Accomack carried the Brandy Clarret and Gin away the Coffee was put into the said Storehouse that the said Goods were landed in about 5 or 6 days after her arrival that at the time of the unlading there were only two hhds of rum and a barl. of Sugar in the said Storehouse one hhd of which belonged to Mr McCroskie the other to Dr. Foushee that he assisted in the unlading the Betsey and that 16 hogsheads of rum part of her Cargo were put on board the Sloop Liberty in about a week after the same had been landed that he carried a bag of Coffee out of the said Storehouse and put it on board the Sloop Liberty and he believes it to be the same that was imported in the Betsey, that when Mr Thorowgood Smith came down to Mr Bowdoin's there were then 13 hogsheads of rum on board the Betsey and that Capt. Sampson the master of the Betsey said that he expected the King's Vessel and ordered the said 13 hhds to be landed which was done and put into the Store with the rest of the Cargo that Capt Sampson after the King's Vessel came in sight ordered the apprentices not to go on board that 2 hhds of Molosses now on board the Betsey are part of her Cargo imported from St. Eustatia that the Marks & Numbers of the rum he believes to be the same as when taken on board in the West Indies but does not know what the marks are, that the deponent cannot read his master having never given him any Learning; that it was near three weeks after the Betsey's arrival before the Liberty came into Hungars Ha[r]bour with Corn which was landed from thence she went to Old Plantation and returned in 4 or 5 days with Oats that upon a signal hoisted on board the Betsey Capt: Sampson directed him to go & see what the boys wanted that when he got on board Mr Locke an Officer of the Magdalen asked if he belonged to the Sloop the deponent answered yes on which Mr Locke told him to go below and then a Signal was hoisted for the Magdalen upon which her Cutter came off and carried the deponent on board the Magdalen; that he received nothing from the Officers but Capt: Collins gave him a pair of Breeches which he was very much in want of that the sloop Betsey was navigated by the Capt: & Apprentices only to the best of his knowledge.

Sworn to in Court
3d. April 1775.
Teste Thos. Everard Register

his
Elligood X Ayres
mark

John Bowdoin Junr. of lawful Age being Sworn Saith That he was present and saw Littleton Savage sign the Certificates now in Court for 16 hhds of Rum that a

Negro Man Stephen on board the Sloop Liberty is a Slave belonging to Severn Eyres Estate decd another Slave on board the Liberty is the Property of John Bowdoin Senr. that Jack another Slave on board the Liberty belongs to Stephen Sampson which Slaves were put on board to Navigate the said Sloop That the Rum laden on board the Sloop Liberty was taken from a Warehouse and not from on board the Betsey That the said Sloop Betsey had the greatest part of her Outward bound Cargo on board at the time the Rum was Shipped on board the Liberty

Sworn to in Court — John Bowdoin Junr:
3d. April 1775

Teste Thos. Everard Register

The Certificate mentioned in this Deposition is inserted after the Respondents Answer.[42]

The Advocate then Exhibited a Libel against the Sloop Betsey and her Lading which had been Arrested by Process sued out of this Court by the said Henry Collins whi[ch Libel is][43] as follows[44]

Virginia scil

Before you John Randolph esq commissary & judge of the court of viceadmiralty in the colony & dominion of Virginia cometh Henry Collins Esq commander of his majesties sloop of war Magdalen who's duly authorised to make seizures & who now prosecutes as well for our sovereign lord the King as himself & gives the court to understand & be informd that on the [ ][45] day of March in the year of our lord 1775 in the port of Accomack in this colony on the high seas & within the jurisdiction of this court he seizd the sloop Betsy whereof Stephen Sampson was late master together with her rigging tackle guns furniture & boats & lading consisting of 15 hundred bushells of corn one thousand bushells of oats & two hhds of molasses for that viz *that* between the day of seizure aforesaid & the first day of January in the year of our lord 1775 the aforesaid corn & oats were laden on board the said sloop Betsy in the port of Accomack to be exported before that bond was given with the conditions securities & penalty as is required by one act of parliament made in the 6 of G. 3 chap 52 intituled an act for repealing certain duties in the British colonies & plantations granted by several acts of parliament &c contrary to the form of the statute in that case made for that viz *that* between the day of seizure aforesaid & the first day of January in the year aforesaid there were imported & brought in the said sloop Betsy into the port of Accomack in this colony 40 hhds containing five thousand gallons of foreign rum or spirits & not rum or spirits of the growth produce or manufacture of any british colony or plantation in America which said foreign rum or spirits being of the produce & manufacture of some colony or plantation in America not under the dominion of our lord the King were unladed & discharg[ed] from the said

[42] In the margin beside Bowdoin's deposition is the direction "after the Deposition enter what follows," namely this statement.

[43] Hole in MS.

[44] MS has "(here enter it)," the libel being a separate document.

[45] Blank space in MS.

sloop Bet[sy as m]erchandise[46] in the said port of Accomac[k][47] contrary to the form of the statute in that case made & provided for that viz *that between* the day of seizure aforesaid & the first day of January in the year aforesaid there were imported & brought in the said Sloop Betsy into the port of Accomack in this colony 36 Cags containing two hundred gallons of certain spirits call'd french brandy 16 cases containing one hundred & fifty gallons of french wine calld claret & 8 cases containing three hundred gallons of certain spirits calld Geneva eight Hds. containing one thousand gallons of Molasses & two hundred pounds of coffee which said spirits & wines are of the growth produce & manufacture of some foreign country in Europe & were not laden on board the said sloop Betsy in Great Britain & imported directly thence into this colony & which said spirits & wines & molasses & coffee were unladed & discharged from the said sloop Betsy in this colony as merchandise before that the master of the said sloop had been to the proper officer for that purpose & reported a true & faithful account of hi[s vessel & h]er[48] lading & paid the duties of the said coffee & molasses contrary to the form of the statutes in that case made & provided for that viz that between the day of seizure aforesaid & the first day of January in the year of our lord 1774 there were laden on board the sloop Betsy whereof the said Stephen Sampson was master in the port of Accomack in this colony 100 hhds containing one hundred thousand pounds of tobacco before that bond was given with the conditions securities & penalty as is required by the acts of trade & before the customs due on the aforesaid 100,000 lb of tobacco were paid to the proper officer for that purpose appointed, which said 100000 lb of tobacco laden as above on board the said Betsy were exported in the said sloop Betsy whereof the said Stephen Sampson was master & unladed in the island of St. Eustatia, which said island of St. Eustatia is a foreign island in America & not a british island or plantation in America contra[ry] to the acts of trade in that case made & provided by means whereof the said sloop Betsy together with her guns &c & her lading &c are forfeited & liable to be condemnd & divided one moiety thereof to our sover[e]ign lord the King the other to the said Henry Collins Esq who prosecutes on this occasion Wherefore he prays the advice of the court in the premisses & that the said sloop [Betsy tog]ether[49] with her guns &c & her lading &c may be condemnd and divided as above.

And on the motion of Thorowgood [Smith on beh]alf[50] of himself and the rest of the Owners of the said Sloop Betsey by George Wythe their Proctor time is given him til Tomorrow [to] put in their Claim and Answer to the said Libel and the Court then adjourned til Tomorrow morning 11 oClock.

4 April 1775

Present John Randolph Esqr.

The said Thorowgood Smith with sufficient Security having Entered into Bond

---

[46] Hole in MS.

[47] Hole in MS.

[48] Hole in MS.

[49] Hole in MS.

[50] Hole in MS.

for Costs the Owners of the said Sloop Betsey and her Lading Appeared and put in their Claim and Answer which is as follows [51]

Before you John Randolph esquire commissary and judge of the court of vice admirality in the colony and dominion of Virginia come Thorowgood Smith John Bowdoin and Preeson Bowdoin merchants a[nd partn]ers[52] owners of the sloop Betsy and the corn oats and molasses on board of her seised by Henry Collins esquire commander of his majestys sloop of war Magdalen and saving to themselves all advantage of exception to the imperfections of the libel by him exhibited against the said sloop Betsy and her lading and not admitting all or any of the allegations in the said libel to be true in manner and form as the same are therein set forth for answer [the]reunto [53] say that before any part of the said corn and oats were laden on board the said sloop Betsy this respondent Thorowgood Smith applied to the officers of the customs of the port of Accomack and acquainted them truly with the then intended voyage of the said sloop Betsy and with the lading she would carry and offered and was ready to do whatever the law required to be done in such cases whereupon the said officers delivered to him a warrant or sufferance to load which sufferance is annexed to the answer of these respondents put in to the libel of the present prosecutor against the sloop Liberty and her lading and which these respondents refer to as part of this answer and these respondents hope if the officers neglected or declined taking a proper bond the vessel and her lading ought not to be subject to forfeiture more especially as the bond in such cases is rarely if ever taken at any custom house in this co[lony as] [54] these respondents have been informed until the master goes to the office to clear out the vessel And these respondents hoping that the said sloop Betsy and her lading may be restored to them pray to be hence dismissed with their costs.[55]

[SUFFERANCE]

Port Accomack

Stephen Sampson master of the sloop Betsey lately arrived from St. Eustatia is hereby permitted to load with Nonenumerated Goods in this district, having made legal Entry. Given under our hands the 17th. February 1775.

D. BOWMAN Naval Officer — FRANCIS MILLER, Comptroller — WALTER HATTON Collector

[ENDORSEMENT]

N.B. the within Sufferance delivered to Mr. Smith 20th. March 1775.

D. BOWMAN

The Libellant Replied thereto Generally and the Court then proceeded to examine the said Elligood Ayres also David Bowman as Witnesses whose depositions are as follow [56]

---

[51] MS has "(here enter it)," the claim and answer being a separate document.

[52] Hole in MS.

[53] Hole in MS.

[54] Hole in MS.

[55] At the end of the claim and answer is the note, in the same hand as the proceedings, "(here enter Sufferance marked C. and the endor[se]ment)."

[56] MS has "(here enter Ayres Deposition and Bowmans 2 Depositions)," the three depositions being three separate documents.

Elligood Ayres Mariner lately belonging to the Sloop Betsey and an Apprentice to Mr. Thorowgood Smith and Co. being Sworn Saith that the said Sloop Sailed from Hungars 3 or 4 days before Christmas last having on board 40 hhds of Tobacco 70 Barrels of Flour or thereabouts as he guessed & 5000 Staves and carried and Landed the said Cargo at St. Eustatia that the said Sloop took on board there 40 Hhds of Rum 36 Cags of Brandy 8 Cases of Gin 16 Boxes of Claret A bag of Coffee about 100 weight and brought the Same into this Colony and Landed the same into Mr. Bowdoins Store House without touching at any Place in their Voiage to this Colony That the said Sloop in August last Sailed from this Colony having on board 46 Hhds of Tobacco 36 Barrels of fish and about 50 barrels of flour all which were Landed at St. Eustatia That the said Sloop also Sailed from this Colony in April 1774 having on board 20 Hhds of Tobacco and a Quantity of Corn the Tobacco was first Landed in St. Eustatia and the Corn at St. Christophers afterwards the Deponent being informed when he mentioned 16 boxes of Claret that it was different from what he deposed yesterday he replied that he then said 16, but being further interrogated declares the Number of Boxes is 14.

The Deponent saith that the Mate and the rest of the Mariners of the said Sloop Betsey are Apprentices to the Owners of the said Sloop.

his
ELLIGOOD X AYRES
mark

The said Ayres further saith that the said Sloop when she returned from her Voiage begun in August last she brought into this Colony 20 hhds of Rum from St. Eustatia and 15 hhds of Rum and 2 barrels of Sugar from St. Christophers.

his
ELLIGOOD X AYRES
mark.

Sworn to in Court
4 April 1775.
Teste THOS. EVERARD Register

David Bowman Naval Officer for the Eastern Shore of this Colony being Sworn saith that the Sloop Betsey cleared out at his Office for the West Indies in the Months of Octr 1773, April 1774 August 1774 and Decr. 1774 with Provisions and Lumber without any Tobacco [That it i]s[57] Customary for Masters of Vessels to give Bond at the Custom House for Non enumerated Goods til the Vessels are Cleared out at the Office. That Vessels frequently Load without a Sufferance and such Vessels are Cleared out without any objection from the Officers. That Mr. Smith is always ready to perform what is required of him to be done by the Officers when he Applys for business to be done in their Offices. That the Custom House is about 26 Miles from Hungars where the Betsey was seised.

D. BOWMAN

[57] Hole in MS.

Deponent further saith that the said Sloop Betsey in August last was Cleared out with 2500 bushels of Corn & 200 bushels of Pease.

Sworn to in Court
4 Apl. 1775
Teste Thos. Everard Register

David Bowman Naval Officer on the Easternshore of this Colony being Sworn Saith that on the 17th. of Febry last Mr. Thorowgood Smith one of the Owners of the Sloop Betsey Entered the said Sloop in the Custom House from St Eustatia with eight Hogsheads of Molasses only and no other Goods or Merchandize whatever a true Copy of the Manifest of the said Sloops Cargo as produced at the time of the said Sloops Entry at the Custom House is now produced in Court.

D. Bowman

Sworn to in Court
4 Apl. 1775.

The manifest mentioned in the said Deposition is as follows [58]

Manifest of the Cargo on board the Sloop Betsey, Stephen Sampson master from St. Eustatia 17th. Feby. 1775.

Eight hhds. containing 800 Galls. Molasses Duty here paid.

Thorowgood Smith

a true Copy
D. Bowman
Naval Officer.

and then the Court adjourned til the tenth of this Instant.

10th. April 1775

Present John Randolph Esqr.

Charles Lyon was produced and Examined as a Witness whose Deposition is as follows (here enter it)[59]

Also Elligood Ayres was again Examined his Deposition is as follows [60]

Elligood Ayres being Sworn Saith that the Voiage in which Charles Lyon was Mate of the Sloop Betsey the Cargo consisted of Corn Pease Oats and some Pork which was landed at Antigua that they went from thence to St. Eustatia and there took on board only a barrel of Bread and some Canvas That the said Sloop has made two or three Voiages from Virginia to St. Eustatia & St. Kitt since Lyon was Mate of her to the best of his knowledge but is [well] [61] satisfied the said Sloop has made at least two Voiages since the said Lyon was Mate that the Cargo from Antigua was Rum and Sugar.

his
Elligood X Ayres
mark.

58 MS has "here enter it," the manifest being a separate document.
59 The deposition is missing.
60 MS has "(here enter it)," the deposition being a separate document.
61 Hole in MS.

Sworn to in Court
10 Apl. 1775
Teste Thos. Everard Register

And by Consent of the Parties the Causes are set for Hearing Tomorrow and then the Court [adj]ourned[62] til Tomorrow morning 10 oClock.

11 April 1775

Present John Randolph Esqr.

And now at this Day the said Causes came on and were partly heard on the Libels Answers and Depositions aforesaid sundry Exhibits produced and read in Evidence and the Arguments of the Counsel on both sides and the Court then adjourned til Tomorrow morning 10 oClock.

12 April 1775.

Present John Randolph Esqr.

The said Causes were this day fully heard and on Consideration of the Libels Answers Depositions and Exhibits aforesaid and the Arguments of the Councel It is Decreed and Adjudged by the Court that the [said Sl]oops[63] Liberty and Betsey together with their Rigging Tackle Apparel a[nd Furniture][64] also 16 hhds of Rum a Bag of Coffee and a Box of Chocolate mentioned in the Libel as part of the Lading of the said Sloop Liberty be condemned and forfeited One moiety thereof to our Sovereign Lord the King and the other moiety to Henry Collins Esqr. the Prosecutor a[nd t]hat[65] the Slaves and Oats on board the Liberty also the Lading of the said Sloop Betsey be acquitted and res[tored t]o[66] the Owners Whereupon It is Ordered that Robert Miller and John C[arter being first sworn befo]re[67] a Magistrate do Appraise in Cur[rent money the said sloops Liberty and][68] Betsey together with their Rigging Tackle Apparel furniture and Goods Condemned That the Marshal after Public Notice given on the Sale thereof at Auction for ready Money[69] and return the Appraisment and an Account of the said Sales to the Court on the 22d. day of this Instant in Order to a final Decree.

22d. April 1775

[Present][70] John Randolph Esqr.

Appraisments in Obedience to the Order of this Court being made and returned are as follow[71]

---

62 Hole in MS.
63 Hole in MS.
64 Hole in MS.
65 Blot on MS.
66 Hole in MS.
67 Hole in MS.
68 Hole in MS.
69 The *Virginia Gazette* (Purdie) for April 14, 1775, advertised the sale, on April 18, at Burwell's Ferry, of the sloop *Betsy* with her rigging, tackle, and apparel, and of the sloop *Liberty* with her rigging etc., sixteen hogsheads of rum, a bag of coffee, and a box of chocolate. The court's order on the notice, appraisal, and sales is garbled but intelligible.
70 Hole in MS.
71 MS has "(here enter Appraisments of the Liberty and Betsey)," the appraisals being two separate documents.

1775	An Appraisment of	
April 18th	The Sloop Liberty rigging &c	£ 65. 0. 0
	16 Hhds of Rum	176. 0. 0
	1 Box Chocolate 40 lbs @ 16d lb	2.13. 4
	1 Bag of Coffee 128 lbs @ 9 d	4.16. 0
		£248. 9. 4

In Obedience to an Order of the Court of Vice Admiralty we the subscribers went on board the Sloop Liberty and· Appraised her and her Cargo as above

ROBT MILLER
JOHN CARTER

An Appraisment of
The Sloop Betsey & rigging
1775 April 18th
In obedience to an Order of the Court of Vice Admiralty we the Subscribers went on board the Sloop Betsey and Appraised her with her Rigging as above.

ROBT MILLER
JOHN CARTER

the Marshal also returned Accounts of the Sales the amount of the Liber[ty][72] and he[r][73] Lading being £318.19.10 and of the Betsey £180 the whole £498.19.10 Current Money The Court then Examined the Accounts of the Charges Expences and C[osts][74] arising in these Suits and allowed for the same against the Liberty £85.18.6 and against the Betsey £54·13/— which two Sums being deducted from the Sales aforesaid remains a balance of £358.8.4 And thereupon It is Decreed and Ordered that the Marshal after paying of the Charges Expences and Costs aforesaid pay to John Earnshaw Esqr. Collector of his Majestys Customs for the Upper District of James River [in][75] this Colony £179.4.2 a Moiety of the aforesaid balance for the U[se of his M]ajesty[76] and to Henry Collins Esqr. the Prosecutor £179.4.2 the other M[oiety th]ereof.[77]

From which Decree as to so much thereof as acquits the Corn and Oats on board the Sloop Betsey and directs the Payment of Charges Expences and Costs out of the Produce of the Sales the said Henry Collins Prays an Appeal to the High Court of Admiralty of Great Britain and the [Respondent also prays an app]eal[78] to the said Court from so much of the [ ][79] Goods as forfeited which Appeals are allowed [ ] Usual in such cases.

[72] Hole in MS.
[73] Hole in MS.
[74] Hole in MS.
[75] Hole in MS.
[76] Hole in MS.
[77] Hole in MS.
[78] Hole in MS.
[79] A piece has been torn from the bottom of the page, and about thirty letters are lost here and later in this sentence.

The Admiralty papers in the Public Record Office have no reference to either appeal, and nothing has been found to suggest that the appeals were actually pressed.

The documents in this case include, in addition to those incorporated in the proceedings, the marshal's account of marks and numbers on hogsheads of rum aboard the *Liberty*, ordered by the court on April 1, and two certificates regarding goods shipped in the *Betsy*. The relevance of the two certificates is not exactly clear, and no mention of either one can be recognized in the proceedings or other documents.

This is the marshal's account of marks and numbers:

The Marks & Numbers of 16 Hhds of Rum on board the Sloop Liberty taken by the Marshal by Order of Court

		Galls.
	No. 8	116.
	3	123 on one Head, the other 125.
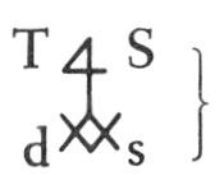	10	118. & 115 on the same Head.
	11	128.
	9	137.
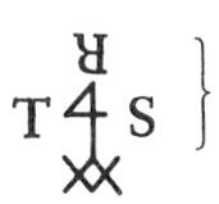	R 6	120.
	11	119.
Do	12	113.
Do	4	112.
Do	9	113. on one Head, the other 111.

T4S dXXS	22	133.	do.	do.	138.
T4S ɑXXS	1	116.	do.	do.	119.
T4S XX	5	114 / 116.			118.
Do	8	109.			
Do	14	124.			
Do	3	122.			

The earlier of the two certificates was perhaps intended to prove that duty had been paid on the molasses mentioned in the deposition by Elligood Ayres of April 3. He supposed that two hogsheads of the molasses were then aboard the *Betsy;* the libel by Collins against the *Betsy* mentioned two hogsheads of molasses as liable to condemnation. This is the certificate:

Port Accomack

T4S XX No. 1 to 7 the eight Cask no Number } This is to Certify all whom it doth concern, that on or about the 17th. Feby last, Thorowgood Smith & Co. imported here in the sloop Betsey, Stephen Sampson master from St. Eustatia, Vizt. Eight hhds Molasses being mark't & number'd as per margin, the duty's of which are here paid. Given under our hands the 25th. day of March 1775.

D: Bowman Naval Officer
Walter Hatton Collector
Francis Miller, Comptroller

The relevance of this last certificate is hard to guess, but it may perhaps concern the grain aboard the *Betsy,* mentioned as subject to condemnation in the libel by Collins:

Virginia Port of Accomack

These are to Certify all whom it doth concern that on the 13th: April 1774 there was clear'd out in the Sloop Betsey Stephen Sampson Master for Antigua Eighteen hundred Bushels of Corn, Thirty barrels Pork, Forty Bls Flour and Thirty bushels Pease; & the said Master then with one Surety gave the Non Enumerated Bond required by act of Parliament which Bond was canceld on the 20th: day of June

1774 [by][80] a Certificate from St: Christophers bearing date 28th: May 1774 containing an [Accoun]t of the landing of the said Articles. And on the 5th Augst: 1774 th[ere w]as cleard out in the said Sloop said Stephen Sampson Master [for] Barbados, Two thousand five hundred Bushels Corn and two hu[ndre]d Bushels Pease. & then also gave a Non Enumerated Bond which was canceld per Certificate from Antigua dated the 4th: October 1774 & Canceld the 2nd: day of Novr: 1774 the said Certificate containing an Account of the landing of the said articles. And on the 1st: day of Decr: 1774 he again cleard out said Sloop for Barbados with Seven hundred & fifty Bushels Corn, one hundred & Sixty three Barrels of Flour, Twenty Barrels Pork and Seven Thousand hhd Staves & then also gave a Non Enumerated & Lumber Bond which was also on the 17th: Feby: 1775 canceld per Certificate bearing date at St: Eustatia the 25th: Jany: 1775 which certificate was sign'd by Two persons supposed to be Merchants there. there also appear'd a Certificate for parts of the Cargoe said to be landed at St Christophers certifying the landing part in St: Eustatia which Certificates being sent to the Honble. Board of Commissioners at Boston with sundry others the date th[ereof] can not be certify'd.

Given under my hand & [seal] the 7th: Apl: 1775

WALTER HATT[ON] Collector

[SEAL][81]

In conclusion, it may be useful to consider a summary comment on the records of the Virginia Court of Vice-Admiralty in the Webb-Prentis Papers, and the other suggestions of the court's activities in 1770-1775 provided by mention or by inference. The records in the Webb-Prentis Papers are apparently a miscellaneous batch of papers, preserved by chance. Other sources of information on the court, meager as they are, demonstrate that those surviving records give a misleading impression of how the court of vice-admiralty in Virginia was occupied during the years 1770-1775. It is true that the records presented here contain documents and proceedings in three ordinary maritime cases, a category to which other sources of information make no reference, but it is likely that many similar cases were heard; and it is obvious that the records of an unknown number of cases involving the trade acts are missing.

The files of the *Virginia Gazette* for 1770-1775 have a few notices of the discharge or acquittal of vessels seized, and many more advertisements of sales of vessels or cargo by decrees of the vice-admiralty court.[82] The reasons for

---

80 These and other letters in square brackets in this document have been lost by a vertical split in the paper.

81 The impression of a seal, stamped in the paper, is barely visible and no details can be discerned.

82 About half of the issues of the Purdie and Dixon *Gazette* for 1770, and about a third of the issues of the Rind *Gazette* for that year are missing. For 1771 and later there are complete files of one or the other of the newspapers.

the decrees are usually not known, except when they are made evident by the court records, or suggested by a list, drawn up by Richard Starke, the advocate, of seizures made in Virginia and condemned by the vice-admiralty court there in the period February-October 1771.[83] If one may judge by the scanty information on the cases, vessels and cargo were most often forfeited and condemned for violations of the trade acts, usually illicit trade or smuggling, but occasionally for failure to obey such regulations as those requiring registers and clearances.

The *Virginia Gazette* (Purdie and Dixon) for July 26, 1770, reported that at a court held that week at the Capitol the schooner *Last Shift,* seized by the *Magdalen,* Captain Collins, was condemned because she had no register, was apparently a French bottom, and for a considerable time had made no entry at a custom house. (What then happened to the schooner is not known.) The *Gazette* added a report that two vessels not named, seized in the Potomac River by H.M.S. *Glasgow,* had been discharged.

Starke's list reveals the seizure in 1771 of nine vessels (two of them later acquitted on payment of costs) and of cargo only from two other vessels: six of the seizures were made by vessels of the Royal Navy, and five by customs officers. Gross proceeds of the sales reached a total of £3,327.6.9 Virginia currency (if one seizure, as it seems, brought no proceeds), with the proceeds of sales ranging from £10 currency for one hogshead of tobacco to £1,134.14.8 currency for a Spanish vessel and what was presumably her stock of provisions. All of the sales were advertised in the *Virginia Gazette,* except that of the sloop *Two Sisters* or *Nonpareil,* probably sold in August or September. The *Gazette* also advertised the sale of the brigantine *Britannia,* not in Starke's list.[84]

The sloop *Mayflower,* and the schooner *Lovely Betsey* with fifteen hogsheads of tobacco, were sold in 1772. The sloop *Sally* and some molasses, sugar, and coffee were sold in 1773. The sloop *Patty,* with corn, tobacco, bread, pease, and flour, was sold in 1774. In 1775 the *Gazette* reported the trial and acquittal with costs of the schooner *Wray Galley,* seized by Captain Collins, and advertised the sale of the schooner *Sally* with tobacco, corn, and oats, and of the schooner *Endeavour* with corn, tobacco, rum, and coffee.[85]

---

[83] See P.R.O., Adm.1/3884, an unnumbered folio, "A List of Seizures . . ." dated November 1, 1771.

[84] *Virginia Gazette* (Purdie and Dixon), February 28; April 11; May 2, 16, 30; June 20; October 10, 24; November 21; December 5, 1771.

[85] *Virginia Gazette* (Purdie and Dixon), February 6, May 7, 1772; August 19, 1773; July 7, 1774; March 10, 17, April 21, 1775.

Thus it is clear that while court records survive from nine cases heard by the Virginia Court of Vice-Admiralty in 1770-1775, Starke's list and the files of the *Virginia Gazette* show that during that period the court heard at least thirty cases. It is impossible to guess how many more cases came before the court in those years, especially ordinary maritime cases bringing no profit to the Crown or the prosecutor, and no obvious interest to anyone except the officers of the court and the parties to the cases. Finally, there is no way of knowing how many breaches of the laws of trade that should have come before the court were undetected, or in any event disregarded by the customs officers.[86]

---

[86] An interesting review of the shortcomings of the customs service in Virginia is in Joseph R. Frese, editor, "The Royal Customs Service in the Chesapeake, 1770: The Reports of John Williams, Inspector General," *Virginia Magazine of History and Biography*, LXXXI (July 1973), 280-318.

INDEX